China
in the World Economy

NICHOLAS R. LARDY

China
in the World Economy

Institute for International Economics
Washington, DC
April 1994

Nicholas R. Lardy, Visiting Fellow, is
Director and Professor of the Henry M.
Jackson School of International Studies at
the University of Washington. He is author
of numerous studies on China's economy.

INSTITUTE FOR INTERNATIONAL
ECONOMICS
11 Dupont Circle, NW
Washington, DC 20036-1207
(202) 328-9000 FAX: (202) 328-5432

C. Fred Bergsten, *Director*
Christine F. Lowry, *Director of Publications*

Cover design by Michelle M. Fleitz
Typesetting by BG Composition
Printing by Automated Graphic Systems

Printed in the United States of America
97 96 95 94   8 7 6 5 4 3 2 1

**Library of Congress Cataloging-in-
Publication Data**

Lardy, Nicholas R.
    China in the world economy /
Nicholas R. Lardy.
        p.   cm.
    Includes bibliographical references and
index.

    1. China—Economic policy—1976—
2. China—Foreign economic relations.
I. Title.
HC427.92.L37   1994
337.51—dc20   94-491
                                                 CIP

ISBN 0-88132-200-8

**Marketed and Distributed outside the USA and Canada by Longman Group UK
Limited, London**

The views expressed in this publication are those of the author. This publication is
part of the overall program of the Institute, as endorsed by its Board of Directors, but
does not necessarily reflect the views of individual members of the Board or the
Advisory Committee.

Contents

Preface

China has clearly become a major participant in the world economy. It is virtually certain to become even more important in the future because of its size, dynamic economic growth, and continuing policy reforms. Yet there is relatively little understanding of many of the fundamental elements of China's emergence, ranging from the actual magnitude of its economy to the extent of its openness to external influences.

Hence the Institute decided to conduct a comprehensive analysis of China's present and potential role in the world economy. Author Nicholas R. Lardy emphasizes the growing integration of China into the world trading system and global capital markets. He also addresses the entire array of economic policy issues now being discussed between China and the United States, including the continuation of most-favored nation status.

This is the fourth such volume that we have produced at the Institute. I personally wrote *America in the World Economy: A Strategy for the 1990s* in 1988. Bela Balassa and Marcus Noland authored *Japan in the World Economy* at about the same time. We released *Korea in the World Economy*, written by former Korean Finance Minister Il SaKong, in 1993. We plan to prepare similar analyses of other key countries and regions as part of our future research program.

The Institute for International Economics is a private nonprofit institution for the study and discussion of international economic policy. Its purpose is to analyze important issues in that area and to develop and communicate practical new approaches for dealing with them. The Institute is completely nonpartisan.

The Institute is funded largely by philanthropic foundations. Major institutional grants are now being received from the German Marshall Fund of the United States, which created the Institute with a generous commitment of funds in 1981, and from the Ford Foundation, the William and Flora Hewlett Foundation, the William M. Keck, Jr. Foundation, the Andrew Mellon Foundation, the C. V. Starr Foundation, and the United States–Japan Foundation. A number of other foundations and private corporations also contribute to the highly diversified financial resources of the Institute. About 16 percent of the Institute's resources in our latest fiscal year were provided by contributors outside the United States, including about 7 percent from Japan. The Rockefeller Brothers Fund provided generous support for this project.

The Board of Directors bears overall responsibility for the Institute and gives general guidance and approval to its research program—including identification of topics that are likely to become important to international economic policymakers over the medium run (generally, one to three years), and which thus should be addressed by the Institute. The Director, working closely with the staff and outside Advisory Committee, is responsible for the development of particular projects and makes the final decision to publish an individual study.

The Institute hopes that its studies and other activities will contribute to building a stronger foundation for international economic policy around the world. We invite readers of these publications to let us know how they think we can best accomplish this objective.

C. FRED BERGSTEN
Director
March 1994

Acknowledgments

The author thanks Mr. Xu Jian for his assistance in gathering much of the material for this study. He wishes to thank the participants in the two study group meetings convened in Washington in the fall and winter of 1993. Those discussions contributed greatly to shaping the final form of the study. The written comments of Richard Cooper, Kimberly Elliott, R. Michael Gadbaw, Harry Harding, John P. Hardt, Kenneth Lieberthal, Jim Lilley, Peter Y. F. Lo, Michael W. Michalak, Wayne M. Morrison, Marcus Noland, Steve Parker, Dwight H. Perkins, Alan Romberg, Susan Shirk, John Williamson, and Paul Wonnacott were particularly helpful in revising the manuscript. The staff of the Institute was helpful in many ways. Christine Lowry and Valerie Norville, in particular, moved the publication and editing process forward in a most expeditious manner. Above all the author wishes to thank C. Fred Bergsten, not only for suggesting the study, but for incisive and detailed comments on each draft of the manuscript.

1

Introduction

At the outset of its economic reforms in the late 1970s, China was an insignificant participant in international markets for goods and capital. In 1977, the sum of its imports and exports, or its total trade turnover, was less than $15 billion, and it was only the 30th largest exporting country in the world. As shown in table 1.1, its share of world trade in that year was only 0.6 percent, significantly less than in 1927–29, when China's trade attained its peak precommunist levels, accounting for a little more than 2 percent of world trade. China's role as a trading nation on the eve of reform also was significantly less than it had been in the 1950s, when the Communist Party launched its ambitious first five-year plan, which was heavily dependent on machinery and equipment imported from the Soviet Union.

Prior to the late 1970s, China also was barely a participant in world capital markets. Except for short-term trade credits, China was not a borrower either in international commercial markets or from international financial organizations such as the World Bank, did not receive foreign aid from bilateral development agencies such as the Japanese Overseas Economic Cooperation Fund, was not a recipient of private foreign direct investment, and did not invest abroad. Finally, the central government fixed the exchange rate at a level that highly overvalued the domestic currency.[1]

The resulting excess demand for foreign exchange was managed through a rigid, highly centralized system of exchange control that

---

1. The Chinese currency is called the *renminbi* and is denominated in yuan, symbolized by Y.

Table 1.1 Merchandise trade, selected years, 1927–93

Year	Billions of dollars	Percent of world trade
1927	1.33	2.1
1928	1.53	2.3
1929	1.44	2.1
1953	2.37	1.5
1957	3.11	1.4
1959	4.38	1.9
1962	2.66	.9
1970	4.59	.7
1975	4.75	.8
1977	14.80	.6
1978	20.64	.9
1980	38.14	.9
1985	69.60	.9
1990	115.41	1.6
1992	165.61	2.2
1993	195.72	2.5[a]

a. Estimated.

Sources: League of Nations, *Statistical Yearbook of the League of Nations, 1930/31*; General Agreement on Tariffs and Trade, *International Trade*; table 2.1.

inhibited China's interaction with the outside world. The Maoist ideology of self-sufficiency, pursued most vigorously in the Cultural Revolution years of the mid- and late-1960s, had left China largely isolated from the world economy.

By the early 1990s China's role in the international economy had been totally transformed. In 1992 China's total trade exceeded $165 billion, accounting for 2.2 percent of world trade. In 1993 turnover was $196 billion, accounting for about 2.5 percent of world trade. As a consequence, China's share of world exports had finally exceeded the previous peak level of the late 1920s. In 1992 it was the world's 10th largest exporter, lagging behind only the largest and most advanced industrial states.[2] It also was a significant recipient of foreign aid and a major

2. According to GATT data, China was the 11th largest exporter in the world in 1992. Hong Kong ranked 10th, just ahead of China. But an unusually large percentage of Hong Kong's exports were reexports of goods produced in China. After adjusting to take this factor into account, China was actually the 10th largest producer of export goods.

borrower on international capital markets. For example, in both 1992 and 1993 it was the single largest borrower from the World Bank and sold large quantities of bonds on international credit markets.

Even more significantly, by the early 1990s China was attracting substantial inflows of foreign direct investment. In 1992 these flows, on a gross basis, reached more than $11 billion, far larger than any other developing country or former communist state. In 1993 actual inflows more than doubled to reach $25.75 billion. Approved foreign investment in 1993 reached the astounding level of $110.85 billion, almost double the level of 1992. Although there is some attrition between approved and actual investment, these data suggest actual foreign direct investment in China will continue to rise over the next few years.

Since reform began, China has made substantial progress toward making its currency convertible. Successive devaluations in the 1980s reduced the degree of overvaluation that was so characteristic of the late 1970s and early 1980s. A rapidly growing, formally sanctioned secondary market for foreign exchange provided additional flexibility for more decentralized trading in goods and services. Since the beginning of 1994, the official rate has been determined in this secondary market, effectively unifying what had been a dual exchange rate system and constituting an important step toward achieving convertibility of the *renminbi* for trade transactions. China also loosened controls on capital flows so that by 1992 it became the source of significant capital outflows.

Over the same period that trade and capital flows registered startling advances, China's domestic economy boomed. From the beginning of reform in 1978 through the end of 1993, real GNP expanded at an average rate of over 9 percent per year so that real output almost quadrupled. By most calculations, this was the fastest growth of any country in the world. China's rate of growth was more than twice as great as the average of all developing economies and even exceeded that of all of the other newly industrializing economies in East Asia, often described as the most dynamic center of economic growth in the world.

By the early 1990s China's rapidly rising economic star had begun to attract significant worldwide attention. Several organizations published new studies of the Chinese economy that evaluated China's real GNP at international prices. These estimates, based on the purchasing power of the Chinese currency, suggested that the Chinese economy had already become, or shortly would become, the third or even the second largest economy in the world. For example, a study of the International Monetary Fund found that on a purchasing power basis the Chinese economy in 1990 accounted for just over 6 percent of world output, ranking third behind only the United States and Japan (*World Economic Outlook*, International Monetary Fund 1993, 117).

The purpose of this study is to examine the implications of China's rise as a major player on the international trade and financial scene. In the postwar period, other countries, notably Japan, achieved a similar meteoric rise. From 1953 through 1973, Japan's imports and exports grew by almost 13 percent annually in real terms (Patrick and Rosovsky 1976, 57). Japan was admitted to the International Monetary Fund and the World Bank in 1952 and became a contracting party of the General Agreement on Tariffs and Trade (GATT) in 1955, when it was the world's ninth largest exporting country. Reflecting its vastly expanded economy and the achievement of the convertibility of the yen, in 1964 Japan became a member of the Organization for Economic Cooperation and Development (OECD), the so-called rich nations' international organization. In 1975 Japan's critical role in the international monetary system was evident in its participation in the first summit of the G-5 nations.

While the world economy has adjusted, more or less, to transformations such as Japan's, China poses three additional challenges. First, its role in the world economy in the 1990s far exceeds that ever played by a communist country. The significance of this will be discussed immediately below. Second, China combines, to an unprecedented degree, large absolute economic size with relatively low per capita income. In the postwar period, no other country with a per capita income as low as China's has played such an important absolute role in the world's trading and financial system. The implications of this will be explored at the end of this chapter. Finally, from the US perspective China is unique—a country combining a global trade deficit with a large bilateral surplus in its trade with the United States. The challenge this poses for US policy will be explored in the concluding chapter.

The Communist Legacy

While the Chinese government, at least in its interaction with the West, attempts to play down the role of Communist Party ideology, China is perceived by many as a historical anomaly—one of the last surviving communist regimes in an era when democracy is commonly perceived to be an ascendent international political force. The accommodation of China's increasing international economic role is all the more difficult because the image of the slaughter of students in Tiananmen Square in Beijing in June 1989 seems indelibly ingrained in the West's collective memory.

Even at their zenith, the Soviet Union and the communist countries of Eastern and Central Europe were minor participants in world trade and finance. Although the Soviet economy was large in absolute terms, its international trade was limited, and of this more than half was with other members of the Council of Mutual Economic Assistance (CMEA). The exports of the Soviet Union to market economies reached a peak of $56 billion in 1988, about 2 percent of world exports. This aggregate figure in some sense overstates the role of the Soviet Union in international product markets since Soviet exports consisted predominantly of crude oil and other raw materials, not manufactured goods that competed with domestically produced goods in the countries importing Soviet goods. At least by 1991, and perhaps as early as 1986, China's exports to market economies exceeded those of the Soviet Union.[3] Moreover, compared with the Soviet Union, manufactured goods comprised a much higher and growing share of China's exports.

Hungary, Poland, and Romania had more diversified trade partners and were more open than China by the conventional criterion of the ratio of exports plus imports to GNP. But, because of the small size of these economies, their annual exports to the West in the 1980s, prior to the collapse of communist political domination, never exceeded a few billion dollars.

Not only was their trade with the West small, before the collapse of communism none of these states had attracted significant amounts of foreign direct investment. In the Soviet Union, for example, the Council of Ministers did not issue the first decree to establish a framework for foreign investment until 1987. Steps to allow majority foreign ownership were taken in 1988, and special tax provisions to attract foreign investment were not enacted until 1990.

The most significant form of economic interaction of the CMEA states with the international economy was borrowing. By the end of 1989, the external debts of these states (excluding Yugoslavia) totaled about $140 billion (Collins and Rodrik 1991, 10). Most of this had been borrowed on commercial terms. However, several Eastern European countries encountered severe balance of payments difficulties beginning in the late 1970s. In 1981 first Poland and then Romania were forced to ask for a rescheduling of their external convertible currency debt. After the imposition of martial law in Poland in mid-December 1981 and the imposition of economic sanctions by the Reagan administration, Western banks

---

3. $56 billion is the product of estimated total Soviet exports of $110.5 billion and the share of exports going to countries that were not members of the CMEA (Collins and Roderick 1991, 9 and 30). The estimate of the total value of Soviet exports is highly sensitive to the prices used to estimate trade within CMEA. Collins and Roderick rely on the estimates of PlanEcon, a private consulting group based in Washington, D.C. The Central Intelligence Agency's estimate of Soviet exports to market economies is much lower, supporting an even more modest assessment of the role of the Soviet Union in the world trading system. The CIA *Handbook of Economic Statistics* (1991, 77) estimates the hard currency exports of the Soviet Union at only $31 billion in 1988, just a little over half the estimate of Collins and Roderick. Based on the CIA's estimate and taking into account the fact that all but a few percentage points of Chinese exports were hard currency exports, China's hard currency exports first exceeded those of the Soviet Union in 1986. There seems little doubt that the margin by which China's hard currency exports exceed those of the former Soviet Union (FSU) widened in the early 1990s. The hard currency exports of the FSU in 1992 are estimated by the World Bank (1993e, vol. 2, 139) at $40.0 billion, less than half the Bank's estimate of the level of 1990 and only around half of China's hard currency exports.

effectively withdrew from further lending to Eastern Europe. Eastern European countries regained access to private international capital markets only gradually, beginning in the early 1990s.

Finally, the Soviet Union and the countries of Eastern and Central Europe were not significant participants in international trade and economic organizations such as the International Monetary Fund, the World Bank, and the General Agreement on Tariffs and Trade. The Soviet Union, far and away the largest of these economies, in fact had no relations with the Fund, the Bank, or GATT, even though it had been an active participant in the discussions in the 1940s leading to their establishment. Poland and Czechoslovakia were founding members of the Fund and the Bank in 1946, before they became centrally planned economies. But the former withdrew in 1950, and the latter was expelled in 1955 (van Brabant 1991, 124–25). In 1972 Romania was the first country in Eastern Europe ruled by a Communist Party at the time of its entry to become a member of the Fund and the Bank. This did not start an immediate trend, since the next Eastern European countries did not join until May 1982 and May 1986, when Hungary and Poland, respectively, became members. However, the World Bank never approved any loans for Poland prior to the collapse of its communist government. Romania discontinued all borrowing from the Bank after 1983.

Only Hungary became a significant borrower from the IMF and the Bank, using two stand-by loans of almost a billion dollars from the former and a loan of almost a half billion dollars from the latter by 1984. The latter loans were combined with approximately $700 million in cofinancing from commercial banks. As a result, Hungary, unlike Poland and Romania, was able to stave off a formal rescheduling of its outstanding hard-currency commercial debt. In the second half of the 1980s, Hungary scaled back its borrowing from the Bank, averaging only a few hundred million dollars annually. Although the Bank's lending was critical for Hungary, it represented only 2 percent of the Bank's annual lending in the second half of the decade. At the end of the Bank's 1989 fiscal year in June, the combined cumulative borrowing of Hungary and Romania was only $4.1 billion, a little more than 2 percent of the Bank's outstanding loans.

The situation with regard to the Eastern European centrally planned economies and the Soviet Union's participation in the GATT was slightly more complex. Czechoslovakia was a founding member. It remained in the GATT continuously after 1948 but participated unobtrusively. Czechoslovakia, for example, did not participate in reciprocal reductions of trade barriers and did not seek to receive most-favored nation (MFN) status in its trade with other contracting parties. Poland, Romania, and Hungary became contracting parties in 1967, 1971, and 1973, respectively. Poland's accession was unusual since it was based not on reciprocal tariff reductions, but rather a pledge to increase imports from other contracting parties—i.e., Western market economies—by 7 percent per year. Poland's economic reform had not yet begun, so its entry was the first of a traditional centrally planned economy. Romania's entry was conditional on its use of planning to ensure that imports from market economies grew at least as fast as total imports during its then-current five-year plan. Hungary's accession came after it had launched its reform, the so-called new economic mechanism. Its entry was accepted as that of a market economy, in retrospect a dubious assumption (van Brabant 1991, 198–206).

Although these three countries were contracting parties of the GATT, their participation was severely constrained. The nature of their trade regimes made it impossible to implement the basic principles of the GATT: reciprocity and nondiscrimination.

China's role in the world economy has already far surpassed that played by the Soviet Union and the communist states of Eastern Europe. Moreover, it is likely to continue to expand. Adjusting to China's increasing international economic role appears to be a particular problem for the United States, especially now that the Clinton administration has embraced the idea that the principal objective of US foreign policy in the post–Cold War era is the enlargement of the world's free community of market democracies (Anthony Lake, speech at Johns Hopkins University School of Advanced International Studies, 21 September 1993). Implicit in this strategy of enlargement is the view that democratization and marketization not only strengthen each other, but that they move forward together.

The formulation of the enlargement strategy advanced by Anthony Lake, President Clinton's national security adviser, seems largely to ignore recent historical experience in East Asia. In South Korea and Taiwan, for example, nondemocratic, authoritarian regimes prevailed until very recently. The development of more democratic regimes in both these states followed several decades of rapid economic growth. That growth was stimulated through economic reforms that expanded the role of the market while reducing the direct role of the state in resource allocation. Democratization followed marketization with a significant lag. Indeed, one could argue that the pressures for political reform stemmed largely from rapid economic growth. Without economic reform it seems doubtful that democratic forces would have become so important in these and some other states in Asia.

The failure to recognize that marketization can ultimately erode the power of authoritarian regimes and create the possibility of an evolution toward more pluralistic political systems has led to a rather strange prescription for US policy toward China. China is grouped in Lake's formulation as one of a small number of "backlash" states, including Iran and Iraq, that pose an explicit threat to what is described as the circle of democracy and markets. This formulation misses the point that the acceleration of China's economic growth, following its dramatic turn toward the market beginning in the late 1970s, was one of the most powerful demonstrations of the bankruptcy of the command economies that at the time still prevailed in the Soviet Union and most of Eastern Europe. China's example perhaps has done as much as anything else to encourage the expansion of market forces in the developing world as well. US policy also misses the point that the best prospect for encouraging the development of a more pluralistic political system in China, one that would have more respect for human rights, may be to encourage the further development of market forces, not to use penalties and sanctions in an attempt to steer China down the path to democracy.

China's Economic Transition Strategy

Although China's reform strategy was premised on increased participation in the international economy, the underlying pace of economic reform in all sectors was constrained by the difficulty of creating markets to substitute for direct government allocation of resources, particularly investment. The summary of progress below suggests that China has had considerable success in expanding the role of the market for goods. Markets for factors of production—land, labor, and capital—have developed more slowly.

Goods Markets

Expanding the role of the market for goods initially was most successful in the farm sector because China had more than 33,000 rural markets on the eve of reform in 1978. Although the Communist Party had led a concerted attack on marketing during the Cultural Revolution and had effectively restricted marketing of such key commodities as grains, the basic structure of rural markets was largely intact. Once the freedom to market was expanded and the state curtailed its traditional dominance of food distribution through the procurement system, rural markets expanded dramatically. Between 1978 and 1992, the number of these markets doubled, and more importantly, the transactions volume soared from Y12.59 billion to Y353 billion. The share of agricultural output sold through the market rose from less than 10 percent of total agricultural output in 1978 to 40 percent in 1992 (*Chinese Statistical Abstract 1993*, State Statistical Bureau, 2 and 97).

Beginning in 1992 in most urban areas, including by May 1993 in Beijing, the system for rationing grain and edible vegetable oil via a coupon rationing system, in continuous use since 1955, was abolished. The retail prices of grain and oils were fully decontrolled. Although price controls were reimposed on these commodities in some cities in the second half of

1993, this was almost certainly a temporary measure taken in response to rising inflation rather than a fundamental reversal of policy.

The role of the market in the distribution of capital goods, such as machinery and equipment, expanded more slowly, largely because the initial conditions were less favorable. Almost without exception, these goods historically had been distributed by the state at fixed prices through its so-called system of materials distribution. Thus, unlike agriculture, there was no preexisting marketing system that could serve as a foundation for further development. But in mid-1984 the state formally sanctioned a two-tier price system for industrial goods, which led over time to a very large role for the market.

The initial idea was a simple one—to provide enterprises with an incentive to raise productivity and output by allowing them to sell their above-plan output on the market. Initially the portion of output sold at market-determined prices was small and subject to a ceiling of no more than 20 percent over the state-fixed price. But in January 1985 the 20 percent limitation was phased out. These marginal prices provided important signals to enterprise managers that led to improvements in resource allocation. Eventually the share of output sold at market prices rose to significant levels, and in the late 1980s and early 1990s the planned prices for most capital goods were eliminated.

In 1992 and 1993 this process even extended to prices of energy and transportation, perhaps initially the most distorted and thus difficult to reform. In the prereform period, coal and crude oil were among the most underpriced commodities in China. In the mid-1980s, when small amounts of above-plan output were sold freely on the market, the ratio of free-market to plan prices for coal and petroleum was among the highest. By 1992 serious reform of the official prices for these commodities was under way. The share that coal producers were forced to sell at low official prices to preferred, state-designated users was dramatically curtailed, the controlled price was raised significantly, and price ceilings, which had been retained on part of above-plan output, were raised. The result was that by the end of 1993 more than three-fourths of all coal was sold at market prices (*China Daily*, 3 November 1993, 2).

Crude oil pricing was somewhat more complex than that for coal, and the pace of reform has been slower. But even here, significant progress has been made. The state reduced the share of planned output sold at the lowest of two official prices from two-thirds in early 1992 to just over a fifth in 1993, more than doubling its price (World Bank 1993b, 50). China is committed to move to a system in which all petroleum is sold at the market price, which already tracks the international price.

Underpricing of transport also has been addressed. The state raised railway freight prices by more than a third in June 1992 (World Bank 1993b, 50). This came on top of a previous doubling of passenger fares on trains, ships, and airplanes in the fall of 1989. These fares had been basically unchanged since the mid-1950s despite the rising cost of providing services, contributing to large operating losses. The price reforms of 1989 and 1992 have gone a long way toward ending the chronic underpricing of freight and passenger transport services, thus enabling the sector to finance badly needed additional investments from retained earnings.

Cumulatively the effect of price reform can be gauged by the declining share of output sold at officially set prices as opposed to market prices. As shown by the data in table 1.2, progress in price liberalization has been most rapid at the retail level. By 1993 only 5 percent of all retail sales were at state-fixed prices. But even the share of capital goods sold at state-fixed prices had declined to less than a fifth by 1993. This progress led the World Bank (1993b, 49–50) to conclude that "the market mechanism now plays the major role in determining commodity prices" and that as a result "commodity price reform can now take a lower profile in the reform agenda."

In a parallel but somewhat delayed fashion, the Chinese authorities transformed the pricing of traded goods. Before 1978, world market prices had almost no influence on the domestic prices of traded goods. On the export side, a handful of monopsonistic foreign trade corporations under the direct control of the Ministry of Foreign Trade purchased goods specified by the plan from domestic producers at officially established prices. The prices of more than 80 percent of all imported goods were set at the same level as comparable domestic goods. Because domestic prices varied widely from world prices, foreign trade companies used the profits they made on some transactions to cover losses incurred on others. This system, in which producers of export goods and users of imported goods were almost fully insulated from changes in world prices, in effect created an air lock separating foreign from domestic prices and greatly distorted trade decisions (Lardy 1992a, 703).

Reforms since the mid-1980s have transformed the pricing of traded goods. By 1991 the domestic prices of well over 90 percent of all goods imported into China were based on world market prices—that is, the domestic price was based on the world price converted to domestic currency at the official exchange rate. The final price was not identical to the world price because import duties, port fees, and other costs were added. But it did mean that domestic prices of these goods changed in response to changes in either world market prices or the exchange rate (World Bank 1993a, 27). In 1991 the state provided financial subsidies for only seven categories of imports that allowed them to be sold at less than world prices. The most important of these were grain, wood pulp, chemical fertilizers, and intermediate products used in producing pesticides (Lardy 1992a, 704). By 1993 the list of subsidized imports had been pared to three, and even these subsidies were scheduled to be phased out in 1994 (*China Daily Business Weekly*, 13 December 1993, 1).

Table 1.2 Share of commodities sold at state-fixed prices,[a] 1978–93

Year	Retail commodities	Agricultural goods	Capital goods
1978	97	94	100
1992	10	15	20
1993	5	10	15

a. Percent is calculated as a share of transaction volume for each category.

Sources: World Bank (1993b, 49–50); Niu Genying (1994, 10).

On the export side, by 1988 the planned delivery of export goods at fixed prices was limited to 21 commodities covering only about a fifth of total export value. Reforms since then have eliminated this mandatory export plan. A decentralization of control of trading led to an increase in the number of companies authorized to carry out trade transactions from about a dozen in 1978 to about 3,700 by August 1991. Increasing competition among these firms, in terms of both price and services, means that for a growing share of export goods, producers receive prices close to world prices. The monopsonistic rents previously enjoyed by the ministry's foreign trade companies have been almost completely eroded.

Markets for Labor

Substantial progress has also been made in expanding the role of the market in the allocation of labor. Particularly in the rapidly growing rural, small-scale industrial sector—the so-called township and village enterprises—the market seems almost fully functioning. Wages appear to be determined in an active market rather than being set according to official state pay scales, as is still the case in much of state-owned manufacturing. By 1993 this sector employed more than 110 million workers and produced a significant share of China's manufactured goods output. In 1990 it produced about $12.5 billion in export goods, a little over 10 percent of China's total exports (Lardy 1992a, 711).

In state-owned manufacturing the role of the market in allocating labor is very much less. There is very little labor turnover, in part because state enterprises have provided such a broad range of benefits and social services to their employees.[4] Of these, the most important are

---

4. As late as 1988, in the entire state sector, including not only manufacturing but other sectors, only 850,000 workers out of more than 99 million left their jobs for reasons other than death or retirement. Thus the annual turnover rate was an astonishingly low 0.8 percent (Lardy 1992b, 123).

pensions and housing. Pensions in the state sector are financed by individual enterprises on a pay-as-you-go basis and are structured so that changing employers has enormous costs in terms of future pension benefits. Most urban housing is controlled by enterprises so that quitting one's job means an immediate loss of housing as well, further discouraging mobility. In addition, a broad range of other benefits and services, including day care, medical care, and sometimes hospital services, is provided in facilities owned and staffed by industrial enterprises. Finally, the state, fearing the political consequences of large-scale urban unemployment, has limited the ability of state-owned firms to reduce overstaffing. Indeed, although the share of manufactured output produced in state-owned firms has fallen significantly since reform began, employment in state-owned industrial enterprises has expanded significantly, from about 31 million in 1978 to just over 45 million at the end of 1992 (*Chinese Statistical Abstract 1992*, State Statistical Bureau, 107; *Chinese Statistical Abstract 1993*, 17).

In short, China has a dual labor market. In rural areas and smaller cities, the market is vibrant, and farmers have been able to shift into manufacturing employment where the terms of employment, wages, and other benefits all are largely market-determined. In the state-owned sector, lifetime employment is still the norm, wages are paid according to national standards, and turnover is low to nonexistent, in large part because of the array of benefits and social services that are tied to employment at a specific firm.

Markets for Land

In the early stages of reform, collectives in the countryside were dissolved, and farmers were provided access to land through leases. Over time, in order to provide more incentives for individual farmers to invest to improve the land, the state increased the length of these leases and made them formally transferable. Although little research has been done on the topic, it appears as though formal transfers of leased land are relatively few, though informal transfers are more frequent. Thus some inefficiencies undoubtedly persist in the allocation of land in rural areas, even though it has been more than a decade since the state has sanctioned markets for leased farm land.

Although less well-known, China has also made dramatic progress in the reform of land and property markets in urban areas. In the last few years, China has introduced land and building rights registration, land leasing, and profit-driven real estate companies, all of which are rare or nonexistent elsewhere in postsocialist economies (World Bank 1993f, 129). Markets are nowhere near as developed as in market economies, but at the margin, market forces are emerging in the urban real estate market. Land increasingly has a value revealed variously by prices in black-market property transactions, prices in officially sanctioned land lease contracts, quasi-market prices such as those involved in reuse and redevelopment projects, and the value of land assets transferred by bankrupt enterprises in the process of merger with profitable enterprises. Land leasing has expanded especially quickly since 1992 in approximately 30 cities where the reform process is most advanced. Thus the World Bank (1993f, 41) concludes that the key issue for China is to expand the scope of explicit market prices for urban land rather than creating such a market from scratch.

Markets for Financial Capital

The least progress has been made in the development of markets for the allocation of financial capital. Superficially it may seem that China has evolved a long way from the period of central planning, when a large share of investment was financed with budgetary allocations. In that era, enterprises surrendered most of their profits to the treasury, which in turn was responsible for reallocating a large portion of these resources to finance fixed investments according to priorities determined in the planning process. Bank loans were only for providing working capital and thus were linked to levels of physical inventories of components and finished goods. By the early 1990s, most investment was financed from a combination of retained earnings and bank loans. Only major infrastructure projects and some key projects in manufacturing were still financed largely through the state budget.

While this structure of financing investment may seem very similar to that found in other mixed economies, a closer examination suggests that the changes have been more modest. Most importantly, the aggregate volume of bank loans is fixed by quotas that central authorities assign rather than in a market with flexible interest rates. Interest rates on bank loans are adjusted, but only infrequently. Banks generally make individual loans not after an assessment of potential risks and returns of projects, but all too frequently in response to demands from local party officials. Since some of the projects so financed turn out to not be economically viable, the banks have accumulated huge portfolios of nonperforming loans that are routinely rolled over. The result of this process has been a significant weakening of the capital position of Chinese banks, all of which are effectively owned by the state. The magnitude of the problem is revealed in the estimates of the World Bank (1992b, 20 and 24) of the overall public-sector deficit. Nominally in 1990 the budget deficit was a modest 1.6 percent of GDP. Inclusive of the deficit of the state-owned enterprises financed through the banking system, the deficit was 11 percent of GDP, almost seven times as high.

In summary, product market reform has proceeded so far that the World Bank no longer regards price reform as a main agenda item.

Progress, on average, in the development of markets for the distribution of land, labor, and financial capital has been more limited. But even within factor markets, progress is variable. Markets already play a substantial role in the allocation of labor, and to a lesser degree even land, in rural areas. The role of urban land markets has been expanding rapidly, particularly since the beginning of 1992. Financial markets are much less developed, and bureaucratic allocation of financial capital appears to remain considerable.

How Large?

While there is little doubt that China's economic reforms have contributed to a substantial acceleration of its underlying economic growth, measuring the level of output in terms of dollars is far more uncertain and thus controversial. This issue gained substantially increased attention in 1993 as the result of a widely publicized report of the International Monetary Fund (*World Economic Outlook*, 1993). Press reports based on this study and other unpublished information apparently provided by the Fund concluded that China's economy was about four times larger than the previous most widely quoted figure and thus only slightly less in absolute size than that of Japan. These and other dollar estimates of China's GDP are contained in table 1.3.

The first three estimates shown in the table are based on the exchange rate—that is, GDP measured in yuan divided by the official exchange rate. The underlying problem of using the official exchange rate is immediately apparent. The World Bank's estimates of 1980 and 1990 per capita income in current dollars are $290 and $370, respectively. Yet the Bank (*World Development Report 1992*, 220 and 268) also estimates that the Chinese economy grew at an annual real per capita rate of just over 8 percent over the same period, implying that real per capita GNP in 1990 should have been more than twice that of 1980. After accounting for price increases in China, which averaged almost 6 percent annually over the period, one would expect 1990 nominal GNP to be about $1,100. Yet the Bank reports a per capita figure of only $370, a third of the expected amount. The explanation is that the Chinese currency depreciated significantly during the 1980s. In 1980 the exchange rate averaged Y1.5 per dollar; by 1990 the average rate was Y4.8. The depreciation cut the World Bank's estimate of per capita GNP by two-thirds.

This distortion is not unexpected. At the beginning of reform, the Chinese maintained a highly overvalued currency. By the end of the decade, the degree of overvaluation had been reduced substantially.

Because of the special uncertainty concerning the meaning of an exchange rate fixed by the government, there has long been an interest among economists in estimating the purchasing power of the *renminbi*.

Table 1.3 Dollar estimates of China's GDP

Source of estimate	Year	Dollars per capita	Total GDP (trillions of dollars)	Share of world GDP
World Development Report 1982[a]	1980	290	.25	n.a.
World Development Report 1992[a]	1990	370	.36	1.6
World Development Report 1993[a]	1991	370	.37	1.6
Lardy (1993, 5)[b]	1990	1,000–1,200	1.14–1.37	5.1–6.1
Asian Wall Street Journal (31 May 1993, 21)[b,c]	1990	1,300	1.47	6.6
New York Times (20 May 1993, A1)[b,d]	1992	1,600	1.66	6.0
World Bank (1992a, 276)[b]	1990	1,950	2.20	9.9
World Bank (1993a, 296)[b,e]	1991	2,040	2.35	10.9
Summers and Heston (1991, 352)[b]	1988	2,308	2.56	15.0
Asian Wall Street Journal (31 May 1993, 21)[b,f]	1990	2,598	2.90	13.0

a. Based on the official exchange rate.

b. Based on the purchasing power of the Chinese currency.

c. An IMF extrapolation of an estimate by Taylor (1991). Taylor's estimate is that China's GDP in 1981 was $417.8 billion. That is equivalent to $410 per capita and is 58 percent greater than the *World Development Report 1993* (152) estimate of $264.34 billion for the same year.

d. An extrapolation of the estimates in the previous row.

e. An update of the estimates in the previous row.

f. Apparently an extrapolation/update of the estimate in the previous row. In 1990 prices.

Such an estimate could, in turn, be used to estimate the real value of China's GNP, measured in dollars.

Estimates of China's GDP based on the purchasing power of the Chinese currency in the early 1990s are shown in the lower portion of table 1.3. They vary widely, from $1,000 to as much as $2,598 per capita. This very broad range underlines the high degree of uncertainty concerning any purchasing power estimate. The basic problem is that the data available for estimating the purchasing power of the Chinese currency are grossly inadequate.

The estimates of China's GDP by Robert Summers and Alan W. Heston (1988, 1991) are the highest of those shown in table 1.3. For 1990 their estimate of $2,598 is fully seven times the commonly cited World Bank figure of $370, which is based on the exchange rate. Summers and Heston's estimates are based primarily on the work of Professor Irving

Kravis (1981). Although Kravis, now deceased, was one of the pioneers in the development of methodologies for measuring purchasing power, he acknowledged that his analysis of China was rough and subject to even larger margins of error than countries formally included in the International Comparison Project (ICP), which he directed for many years. First, the set of commodity price data Professor Kravis was able to collect for China was quite small, fewer than 100 commodities compared with the 300–500 prices for most of the ICP country studies. Moreover, the sample for China included relatively few producer goods prices. Second, estimating the breakdown of GDP expenditures was unusually difficult since at the time of Kravis's work the Chinese published data on aggregate output still were based on the old Soviet concept of net material product (NMP) rather than the Western concept of gross national product. Even the NMP data were not available in sufficiently disaggregated form.

The most recent estimate published by Summers and Heston (1991) is based in part on some additional 1986 price data. But it is difficult to judge the reliability of their current estimates since they have not published anything about the 1986 price sample.

The purchasing power estimates of China's GDP of the World Bank are well below those of Summers and Heston. For 1990 the Bank's purchasing power parity estimate is a little more than five times the estimate based on the exchange rate. The Bank generally relies on ICP estimates where they are available. But since China has not participated in the ICP, the Bank publishes its own estimate. None of the details of this estimate is available, but the Bank warns in a footnote that it is "subject to more than the usual margin of error."

The IMF estimate published in 1993 is based on an earlier study of Jeffrey Taylor (1991). Taylor's analysis is based on relative price ratios for more than 200 commodities, the largest published set of any study, and China's 1981 input-output table. He revalued intermediate flows in the input-output table in dollar terms using average dollar-yuan price ratios calculated for each of the 24 sectors in the input-output table. He then subtracted these intermediate flows from the gross value of output of each sector, also measured in dollars, to produce value-added estimates for each of the sectors. Finally, Taylor summed these estimates to get an estimate of China's GDP.

Since the benchmark estimate is for 1981, Taylor generated estimates for prior and subsequent years by applying official data on the real growth of the primary, secondary, and tertiary components of GDP to his estimates of the base-year output of each of these components. This procedure led him to a GDP estimate of $868.48 billion in 1989, measured in 1981 prices. The implied real growth rate for 1978–89 is 8.6 percent, half a percentage point below the official data. The reason for the difference is that the dollar weights of the primary, secondary, and tertiary sectors differ from the yuan-weighted values used by the Chinese.

The IMF's estimate of a $1,300 per capita income in 1990, which does not appear in its published study but is attributed to IMF officials in the 31 May 1993 *Asian Wall Street Journal*, appears to be an update of Taylor's estimate of 1989 output measured in 1981 dollars. But the separate adjustments for prices and real output have not been published. The IMF estimate of China's real GDP in 1990 is three and a half times the World Bank's exchange rate estimate.

Although Taylor's methodology appears to be stronger than that of Summers and Heston, it is far from airtight. As Taylor suggests, it would benefit from more refined yuan-dollar price ratios, a further disaggregation of the official constant-price GNP growth rates used to project the estimated level of output forward and backward from the benchmark estimate, and the use of a later, more detailed input-output table, such as the one the Chinese compiled for 1987.

Given the weaknesses of the studies summarized above, there is some advantage to using somewhat simpler methods to estimate China's real GNP. One, undertaken by Ma and Garnaut (1992), is to systematically compare patterns of food consumption in China with those that occurred historically in Taiwan. The key point of comparison is the year in which incomes rose to such a high level that the direct consumption of grain began to fall. In Taiwan this occurred in 1961, when the direct per capita consumption of grain reached a peak of 190 kilograms annually. Since then, direct grain consumption has trended downward while the consumption of more expensive foods such as red meat, poultry, eggs, seafood, and milk has continued to rise.

In China, since incomes were quite low, direct food grain consumption rose markedly in the early years of reform. However, direct grain consumption hit an almost identical peak of 187 kilograms in the mid-1980s and has since gradually declined while consumption of meat, poultry, eggs, and so forth has continued to rise.

Since the exchange rate estimate of China's per capita income when direct grain consumption hit a peak in 1987 is $260 while Taiwan's 1961 per capita income (in 1987 prices) was $850, the comparison suggests that China's real per capita GNP in 1987 was a little over three times that calculated using the official exchange rate.

Ma and Garnaut's more detailed comparisons (1992, 13) of the income-consumption profiles for poultry, red meat, eggs, and so forth lead to the same conclusion: "The overall level of consumption of high-value foods enjoyed by an average Chinese consumer in the late 1980s already reached Taiwan's levels in the mid-1960s." The income-consumption profiles are similar if China's per capita income is multiplied by a factor of three.

Another simple approach that also yielded an estimate of a per capita income of approximately $1,000 in 1990 is that of Perkins (1992). He compared per capita output of a handful of important products such as electric power, steel, grain, and cotton yarn in China and South Korea and concluded that by 1990 China's per capita output likely was roughly at the level South Korea had achieved in the late 1960s. South Korea's per capita income in the late 1960s had just passed $1,000 (in 1991 prices), a level he accepts as a reasonable approximation for China as well.[5]

The conclusion of this analysis is that a prudent estimate of China's real per capita income in 1990 is about three times the exchange rate–based estimate—something around $1,100 per capita. Based on that per capita estimate, in aggregate terms China's 1990 GNP would be $1.25 trillion. Based on the IMF's purchasing power estimates of output for other countries, China would rank third—well behind the United States, three-quarters the level of output of Japan, but well ahead of Germany and other major industrial countries.

What are the implications of this estimate for measurements of the openness of the Chinese economy? Based on China's trade turnover of $115.5 billion in 1990, China's trade ratio—that is, its exports plus imports as a percentage of GNP—was a little over 9 percent. By contrast, if one believes that China's real per capita GNP in 1990 was as high as $2,598 (table 1.3, last row), one has to also believe that China's trade ratio in the same year was only 4 percent and that exports constituted just slightly more than 2 percent of GDP. The latter figure seems extraordinarily low, even taking into account China's large population and relatively ample supplies of many raw materials. The high-end estimate of China's per capita real GDP would suggest that the role of foreign trade in China's recent economic transformation has been trivial—a conclusion not reached by any study of China's economic reforms.

China's Growth Prospects

While I do not believe that the Chinese economy is as large as the IMF estimate suggests, what are the prospects for economic growth over the remainder of the 1990s? A comparison with the other high-performing economies in East Asia suggests that China should experience rates of economic growth that are well above the world average. In short, China has a reasonable prospect of sustaining rates of growth of about 6 percent.

If further financial, fiscal, and related measures discussed later in this chapter are implemented successfully, Chinese economic growth until

5. Both the estimates of Ma and Garnaut and of Perkins must be regarded as suggestive rather than definitive. Most importantly, they are based on an extremely small number of commodities, which may or may not be representative of the Chinese economy as a whole. Moreover, the figures for Taiwan's income in 1961 and South Korea's in the late 1960s were calculated on an exchange rate basis. A further adjustment to put them on a purchasing power parity basis would be needed to make a more meaningful comparison.

the turn of the century might even match the 9 percent annual rate of expansion achieved in 1980–93.

This conclusion is based on an analysis of those factors that the World Bank (1993c) believes are important in explaining high growth in the eight high-performing Asian miracle economies. But it is tempered by a recognition of the importance of the productivity gains that underlay much of the expansion of the 1980s and the judgment that without further significant reform steps, future gains in total factor productivity are likely to be quite modest. More importantly, the conclusion also is based on the judgment that the transition to a post–Deng Xiaoping leadership in China will not have a significant disruptive effect on economic growth. If this is wrong and there is a protracted and highly disruptive political succession, economic performance could deteriorate to a rate significantly below that predicted here.

Strong Agricultural Foundation

Reforms of China's agriculture beginning in the late 1970s led to an unprecedented spurt of growth of agricultural output and productivity. Between 1978 and the mid-1980s, the rate of growth of agricultural output was several times the long-term historical rate, and total factor productivity rose sharply. Moreover, taxation of the agricultural sector, particularly indirect taxation, fell sharply, further enhancing the growth of rural household incomes.

Because China's land per capita ratio began from less favorable conditions than other rapidly growing economies in Asia, one might anticipate that the decline in the share of employment in agriculture would be slower. Indeed, the share of employment in agriculture has declined from about three-quarters at the outset of reform, but at almost three-fifths in 1992 it is still quite high. In any case, higher agricultural incomes have allowed higher rates of saving among the rural population. That was a principal factor contributing to a rising rate of household saving in the 1980s.

High Rates of Saving and Investment

China's rate of saving and investment as a percentage of GNP has long matched those of the high-performing economies in East Asia. But in the prereform period, as in other centrally planned economies, almost all saving was government saving—the difference between tax revenues and current government expenditures. Since 1978, the source of saving in China has changed dramatically. Total household bank savings were only 6 percent of GNP in 1978 but had shot up to 46 percent by 1991. As a result, the household share of total savings rose from less than a fourth in 1979 to almost three-quarters by 1991 (Qian 1993). Most of this was mobilized through the state-owned banking system and has been lent to the enterprise sector, mostly to state-owned firms. Where China obviously still differs from the other high-performing economies in Asia is that a very large, though declining, share of investment remains public.

Effective Human Capital Formation

China, like the other rapidly growing economies in East Asia, has emphasized primary and secondary rather than tertiary education. As a result, literacy rates are unusually high for China's level of per capita income. Literacy has been a major factor facilitating productivity gains in the rapidly expanding industrial sector of these economies in their early growth.

Relatively Low Income Inequality

Even prior to reform, life expectancy in China was somewhat higher than would be anticipated based on its level of per capita income. In part this was due to successful public health measures taken in the 1950s that substantially reduced the incidence of infectious and parasitic diseases that were significant causes of premature death in China prior to 1949. But it was probably also due in part to relatively modest income inequality.

The gains from accelerated economic growth during China's economic reform have been broadly shared. In part this is a result of the spurt of agricultural growth that characterized the first six or seven years of economic reform. According to a World Bank study (1992a), China in this period succeeded in lifting a larger share of its absolutely poor population out of poverty in a shorter period than any other nation. The study estimates that in 1978, 270 million Chinese, overwhelmingly rural, lived in absolute poverty—a level linked to a subsistence diet of 2,150 calories per day with extraordinarily low levels of expenditure on non-food items. By the mid-1980s this number was reduced to just under 100 million. Thus the share of China's population living in absolute poverty declined from about one-third to less than a tenth. Reduction in the extent of absolute poverty also was accompanied by increasing life expectancy and falling mortality rates.

Estimates of the degree of inequality in rural China in the early 1990s and how this compares with the late 1970s are subject to many of the same uncertainties that apply to the measurement of income inequality in other developing countries. The World Bank has done more work on this subject than any other organization. Their estimates show that rural income inequality, as measured by the Gini coefficient, fell sharply between 1978 and 1982, presumably as a result of the substantial alleviation of absolute poverty, discussed above. Inequality then rose between 1982 and 1985 but was essentially unchanged between 1985 and 1990. After more than a decade, rural inequality was slightly less than it had been at the outset of reform, a remarkable achievement given the acceleration in the rate of growth of rural output and income (Khan et al. 1992, 1056; World Bank 1992a, ix).

Based on the World Bank's estimates, rural inequality in China is substantially below that in Bangladesh, India, Indonesia, Thailand, the Philippines, and South Korea and comparable to that in Taiwan. However, the estimate of rural inequality of Khan et al. for the single year 1988 is somewhat higher than that of the Bank. They argue that China compares favorably with Southeast Asian countries but has no less and in some cases more inequality than other East Asian countries (Khan et al. 1992, 1056–59).

Urban inequality in China at the end of the decade of the 1980s was very substantially below that in other Asian countries for which data is available (Khan et al. 1992, 1056).

Rapid Demographic Transition

China, like other high-performing economies in East Asia, has undergone a rapid demographic transition—the shift to low-fertility, slow population growth. Evidence of the relatively early transition was apparent even prior to the onset of economic reforms. China's annual population growth in the 1970s was only 1.8 percent, well below the average of 2.5 percent per annum of all other low-income economies. In the 1980s, China's population growth rate fell further, to 1.5 percent, while the average rate among other low-income economies fell only slightly to 2.4 percent. Declining fertility leads initially to higher rates of saving, boosting economic growth.

Where China differs is that part of the transition has been because of coercive government family planning policies such as the unpopular one-child norm, forced abortions, and forced sterilizations. Elsewhere in East Asia, the demographic transition is explained by rising incomes, growing urbanization, increased female labor-force participation rates, and other social and economic factors rather than direct government intervention. Coercive family planning policies in China constitute part of the concern about China's human rights regime, discussed further in chapter 5.

Rapid Growth of Manufactured Exports

As will be discussed in chapter 2, the growth of China's manufactured exports has been quite rapid since 1978. Between 1985 and 1993, the growth was extraordinary, almost 24 percent per annum. As a result, China dramatically increased its share of world manufactured goods exports from 1.2 percent in 1985 to 2.1 percent in 1991. That pace of penetration of world markets in manufactured goods, if sustained for another decade, would compare favorably with the increase from 1.6 percent in 1965 to 5.7 percent in 1980 by the high-performing East Asian economies, not including Japan, whose increased share of manufactured exports was proportionately much less than that of the others during that period (World Bank 1993c, 38).

High Productivity Growth

In the high-performing economies of East Asia, the rapid growth of manufactured exports, combined with policies on human capital creation, led to high rates of growth of total factor productivity. The World Bank (1993c, 317) hypothesizes that this is because exports help economies adopt and master international best-practice technologies. At the firm level, labor with high levels of cognitive skill is better able to adopt, adapt, and master technology. "Thus, exports and human capital interact to provide a particularly rapid phase of productivity-based catching up."

Many believe that a similar process has been under way in China since the late 1970s. There is no doubt that total factor productivity has grown rapidly in agriculture and in township and village, urban collective, as well as private enterprises, which by 1992 accounted for about half of manufactured goods production. Even among the somewhat lethargic state-owned enterprises (SOEs), total factor productivity may have increased significantly during the 1980s. A recent Bank study, which surveyed a large number of studies on the subject, concluded that the best estimate is that total factor productivity in SOEs grew at an annual rate of 2.5 percent in 1980–88 (Harrold forthcoming, 50).

China as a High-Performing Economy

The similarities between China and the high-performing economies in East Asia suggest that China's rapid growth of the 1980s and early 1990s was not an anomaly. There are, however, important differences that strain the analogy. Arable land per agricultural worker in China is considerably lower than elsewhere in Asia, even lower than in Bangladesh. This makes sustaining an adequate rate of agricultural growth a greater challenge. This may be an important factor explaining the slower growth of agricultural output since the mid-1980s compared with the first six or seven years of reform.

Equally important, the extent of public ownership and the share of public investment is much higher in China than in the high-performing economies of East Asia. A significant share of China's publicly owned enterprises, after a decade and a half of reform, still require massive subsidies in order to cover their financial losses. As outlined in the discussion above on China's economic transition strategy, in recent years most of these subsidies have been provided not through the state budget but through loans from state-owned banks. Since these loans, which constitute a significant share of the banks' assets, are nonperforming, China's state-owned banking system is for all practical purposes bankrupt.

Reforms of the financial system endorsed by the Chinese Communist Party in the fall of 1993 envision isolating these nonperforming loans in a newly created long-term credit bank or policy bank and converting existing banks to operate on commercial principles. However, China's banking system has limited experience or immediate capacity to allocate credit rationally. Moreover, given the reluctance of the Communist Party to allow the creation of private banks, one can at least question the ability of reformed, but still state-owned, banks to operate on commercial principles. So the payoff from the commercialization of state-owned banks may not be evident for some time. Finally, after the creation of the policy bank, the existing specialized banks will have to be recapitalized before they can begin operation on commercial principles. Because the operating profits of these banks are minuscule (World Bank 1993a, table 6.1), it seems unlikely that they would be able to raise new capital by selling shares, even if the state were willing to reduce its ownership. Thus recapitalizing the banks will almost certainly be a substantial drain on government fiscal resources that, at the margin, will slow future economic growth.

Another major difference between China and some of the high-performing economies in East Asia is that China has been far more dependent on foreign capital to generate exports, particularly of manufactured goods. As will be discussed in detail in chapters 3 and 5, most of China's manufactured exports are produced by foreign-invested firms[6] or by Chinese firms with close ties to foreign firms. Most of the latter appear to be township and village enterprises or other firms that are not state-owned. In 1992 and 1993, for example, foreign-invested firms, which account for only a few percentage points of China's output, were the source of about two-thirds of the expansion of exports.[7] Much of the rest of the increase came from export processing, which appears to be largely the domain of township and village enterprises. State-owned firms, which in 1992 accounted for about half of manufactured goods output, have been only modest contributors to the expansion of

---

6. The term "foreign-invested firm" encompasses equity joint ventures, contractual joint ventures, and wholly foreign-owned firms.

7. Calculated on the basis of data in tables 2.1 and 3.9.

China's exports. Thus it would appear that China has been less successful than the high-performing economies in East Asia in linking the rapid
growth of manufactured exports with high rates of growth of total factor
productivity. A large portion of China's industry may not be participating in the process at all.

A final major difference between China and the high-performing
Asian economies is income distribution. While the benefits of accelerated growth in the first decade or so of reform were shared broadly,
China is still marked by substantial income inequalities that could
undermine support for continued reform. Most importantly, the gap
between urban and rural living standards continues to be very much
wider than elsewhere in Asia. Indeed, the gap is so great that even
though levels of urban and rural inequality in China, measured separately, are below those elsewhere in Asia, China's overall income
inequality exceeds that in Taiwan and South Korea and is comparable to
that observed in several South and Southeast Asian countries (Khan et
al. 1992, 1056). In addition, growing corruption may be perceived as a
significant source of income inequality. It may reduce societal tolerance
for inequality, even if in certain dimensions the distribution of income is
no more or even less unequal than in other developing countries.

Assuming that China is able to institute the further reforms required
to address income inequalities, to reduce or at least contain corruption,
and to generate sufficient productivity gains to sustain a rate of growth
of about 9 percent per annum, what are the implications for the future
magnitude of total economic and per capita output? How realistic are the
extrapolations that predict China will become the world's largest economy by 2010 (*The Economist*, 28 November 1992, 5)? *The Economist*'s
prediction was based on the per capita income figure of about $2,600
shown in table 1.3. If China's 1990 real per capita income was $2,600 and
the overall economy continued to grow at a rate almost four times that of
the United States, *The Economist*'s prediction would be proved correct.[8]

However, in my judgment it is a dubious prediction on two grounds.
First, as already discussed, it seems more likely that China's level of per
capita output in 1990 was about $1,000, not the much higher figure
underlying *The Economist*'s projection. More important, straight-line
extrapolations over long periods are rarely correct. Even if China were
able to institute the ambitious agenda discussed above, which would be
necessary to sustain a 9 percent rate of growth through the remainder of
the 1990s, it is likely that by the turn of the century or shortly thereafter
China's growth rate relative to that of the United States would begin to
decline. Under the optimistic scenario, by the turn of the century China
would have sustained a 9 percent average annual rate of growth for

---

8. Based on growth rates of 2.3 and 8.7 percent per annum for the United States and
China, respectively.

almost two and a half decades. Experience suggests that sustaining such a supercharged growth rate for more than 25 years is rare.

On the more realistic assumptions that China began from a per capita income of $1,000 in 1990 and that the growth differential relative to the United States drops from almost 4-to-1 to 2-to-1 after 2000, China's output would not surpass that of the United States until around 2040.

Even then, because of its large population, per capita output would be relatively low. If China enjoyed its per capita growth differential of just more than 5-to-1 from 1990 to 2000 and then was able to sustain a 2-to-1 per capita growth differential indefinitely, it would not surpass the United States on a per capita basis until near the end of the 22nd century.[9]

Even if China is unable to sustain the reforms necessary to generate the productivity gains that are required to achieve a rate of growth averaging as high as 9 percent annually through the rest of this decade, the essential story remains the same. If China's growth for the remainder of the century is the alternative 6 percent rate and then follows the pattern relative to the United States that is sketched out above, China would still be the world's largest economy by the middle of the next century. But its huge population means that its per capita income would still be relatively low.

In the eyes of some, these long-run predictions for China are irrelevant. In their view, China is politically so fragile that it constitutes a threat to internal stability, which could undermine future growth. The most extreme scenarios posit regional fragmentation, even a return to a situation similar to the late 1910s and the 1920s, when regionally based warlords exercised de facto control of large portions of China's territory.

Regional Fragmentation

While one can not rule out the possibility of China fragmenting into autonomous or quasi-autonomous regions, for several reasons the prospects for such disintegration seem low. Above all, China is not divided by historical, religious, racial, and other cleavages that have been so important in the disintegration of the Soviet Union and Yugoslavia. China is populated overwhelmingly by those of the Han race. Minorities constitute a significant portion of the population only in the Northwest and in parts of the Southwest. The increased political autonomy of Kazakhs, Uighurs, and other minorities in the republics of the former Soviet Union undoubtedly fuels the political aspirations of the same minority peoples on the Chinese side of the border. But this has been tempered by the recognition that rapid economic growth in China has

---

9. Based on per capita growth rates of 1.4 and 7.3 percent per annum for the United States and China, respectively.

brought enormous improvements in welfare and living standards in China, even in China's relatively remote Northwest, while the opposite trend is evident in adjacent areas of the former Soviet Union.

Not only is China overwhelmingly populated by Han people, since the unification of China in 221 BC they have subscribed to the ideal of the unity of China. While this has not always been achieved, China was effectively unified for most of the Ming and Qing dynasties (1368–1911). The ideal of a unified Chinese state continues to exert a powerful appeal.

Finally, in economic terms it would appear that China is becoming more regionally integrated and that the economic cost of any one province going it alone has increased significantly in the last decade. Most of those who argue that regional fragmentation is likely believe that it will be the rich coastal regions that will break away. But an examination of the economically most successful province, Guangdong, suggests that the economic gains from independence are far from obvious.

Guangdong's economy has flourished under reform, growing about a third again more rapidly than the national average. Its success in foreign trade is legendary. Between 1985 and 1992, it doubled its share of China's exports and since 1986 has widened its lead as China's number-one exporting province. Given the dominance of adjacent Hong Kong as the main source of foreign investment in China, Guangdong also is the site for a very large share of China's total foreign direct investment. By almost any measure, the province, with a population of 65 million, is more integrated into the world economy than any other. In short, in the eyes of some it is a leading candidate for going it alone.

What has been less noticed is the degree to which the province has also become increasingly dependent on the rest of China, both as a source of raw materials and as a market for finished goods. Guangdong exports a higher share of its manufactured goods than any other province—one-third. It consumes another third itself, leaving another third that is "exported" to other provinces. Provinces to the north, such as Hunan, in the mid-1980s tried both to keep Guangdong's finished products out and to keep its own agricultural products and raw materials from flowing to Guangdong. But after evidence accumulated that local protectionism was slowing economic growth and limiting improvements in living standards, Hunan began more fully opening its borders beginning in 1990. Today, Hunan and other provinces are working to strengthen their transport links to Guangdong, to further open channels for domestic trade.

At the same time, there has been a substantial increase in interprovincial capital and even labor flows since economic reform began. The three special economic zones in Guangdong, particularly Shenzhen, have attracted significant amounts of capital from interior regions (Yukawa 1992). Virtually all provinces opened special offices in Shenzhen, and many established manufacturing enterprises as well. Given Shenzhen's relatively liberal system for providing residence permits, the managers and staff of these new enterprises typically come from the investing province (Vogel 1989, 140–43). At the same time, companies in the zones have invested hundreds of millions of yuan annually in developing sources of raw material supplies in inland areas.

The Guangdong provincial government itself is making substantial investments in electric power generation and transmission facilities in other provinces. The province is investing particularly in hydropower development in the Southwest. A number of projects, including the Tianshengqiao and Longtan Hydropower Plants on the Hongshui River, which flows across the Guangxizhuang Autonomous Region, are being undertaken by the South China Joint Hydropower Company. The company, established in 1988, is a joint effort of Guizhou, Guangdong, and Yunnan Provinces, the Guangxizhuang Autonomous Region, and the State Energy Investment Company, a unit of the Ministry of Energy Resources in Beijing. The development of the Tianshengqiao and Longtan hydroelectric power stations also is supported with World Bank loans. The Tianshengqiao plant, with a capacity of 2.52 million kilowatts, was linked to the Guangdong power grid via a 500-kilovolt power line in July 1993. Guangdong Province also is putting up 60 percent of the capital for hydropower development in Yunnan's Lancang River and apparently will bear most of the cost as well of building facilities to transmit the power across Guangxi into Guangdong Province. In combination with three other provinces, Guangdong is also investing in thermal power generation facilities in the Southwest and the high-capacity transmission lines to bring the power east to Guangdong.

In short, just as reform has led to China's greater integration into the world economy, the increasing marketization of the domestic economy has led to increased internal economic integration. While this does not necessarily preclude the rise of forces of regional separatism, it makes them much less likely.

Summary

China already plays a major role in the world economy. In the space of a little over a decade it has emerged as a major trading country and a significant participant in international capital markets as well. On the basis of a relatively cautious assessment of its level of output and its growth prospects, it already does and will continue to combine a large GNP and a low per capita income to a degree unprecedented for a major participant in the international economy.

India is the only country that even approaches this status. On a purchasing power parity basis, its GNP surpasses all but that of China and a very few advanced industrial countries. But in most respects, India has not yet become a major participant in the world economy. Its external debt in 1992 was only slightly less than that of China, partly because its debt outstanding to the World Bank is more than twice as great. But in 1992 its exports were less than a third of China's. And despite economic reforms of the early 1990s, India in 1992 received only about one one-hundredth as much foreign direct investment as China. China's sales of bonds and equities on international markets in 1992–93 similarly dwarf those of India (World Bank 1993e vol. 1, 123–24 and 133; vol. 2, 90–91 and 206–07).

These circumstances, and the fact that China's role in the world economy far exceeds that ever previously played by a communist country, considerably complicate the world's adjustment and accommodation to China's economic transformation. As already suggested, US government policy in particular seems unable to adjust to and deal effectively with a country that combines substantial use of market forces with a communist political system. As will be discussed further in chapter 5, China's already large exports and even greater future export potential are reasons that its trade system is being subject to an unusually high degree of scrutiny in discussions of its participation in the GATT. It is likely that if China were an average-size, low-income developing country with modest exports to market economies, comparable to, say, Polish exports of just under $1 billion at the time of its accession in 1967, it would have been admitted to the GATT some years ago.[10]

---

10. Poland's total exports in 1967 were $2.526 billion, of which only 38 percent or $960 million were to developed-market economies or developing economies (GATT, *International Trade*, 1969, 278).

2

China and the World Trading System

The market and price reforms described in the previous chapter stimulated the dramatic surge in Chinese foreign trade in the reform era. As reflected in table 2.1, with the single exception of 1982, China's trade turnover has increased in every year since reform began. Exports and imports have each expanded at an annual average rate exceeding 16 percent. Domestic economic reforms also caused important changes in the direction of trade and in the commodity composition of trade, particularly in China's exports.

Commodity Composition

Economic reforms in China, particularly the reforms in the pricing of traded goods analyzed in the previous chapter, eventually led to substantial changes in the commodity composition of China's exports. Even before China's economic reform was visible to the outside world, Deng Xiaoping in the mid-1970s was formulating a strategy for opening up China's economy that was highly dependent on increased exports of coal, petroleum, and petroleum products. Deng was vigorously attacked for articulating this strategy of opening, particularly because of its dependence on energy exports. This attack was one of the factors that led to his political eclipse in 1976 and early 1977, and it illustrates the controversy that surrounded China's initial turn toward the outside world and the fragility of Deng's position.

After Deng was restored to power in the spring of 1977, his economic strategy for opening up the economy was resuscitated. Between 1977

Table 2.1 Foreign trade, 1978–94[a] (billions of dollars)

Year	Exports[b]	Imports[b]	Balance
1978	9.8	10.9	−1.1
1979	13.7	15.7	−2.0
1980	18.1	20.0	−1.9
1981	22.0	22.0	0
1982	22.3	19.3	+3.0
1983	22.2	21.4	+.8
1984	26.1	27.4	−1.3
1985	27.4	42.3	−14.9
1986	30.9	42.9	−12.0
1987	39.4	43.2	−3.8
1988	47.5	55.3	−7.8
1989	52.5	59.1	−6.6
1990	62.1	53.4	+8.7
1991	71.9	63.8	+8.1
1992	85.0	80.6	+4.4
1993	91.8	104.0	−12.2
1994, forecast	108.0	116.0	−8.0
Memo items:			
Rates of growth (percent per year)			
1978–93	16.1	16.2	
1980–93	13.3	13.5	

a. Data for 1978 and 1979 were compiled by the Ministry of Foreign Economic Relations and Trade. Data for 1980 and subsequent years were compiled by China's General Administration of Customs. The data from these two agencies differ in coverage, valuation, and recording times (Lardy 1992b, 12–13).

b. Imports are valued at c.i.f. prices, exports at f.o.b prices.

Sources: State Statistical Bureau, *Chinese Statistical Abstract 1993*, 101; New China News Agency, *People's Daily*, 10 January 1994, "China's Foreign Trade Increases to Reach $195.7 Billion"; *China Daily Business Weekly*, 3 January 1994, "China to Slow Down GDP Growth."

and 1985, China's annual exports of crude oil and refined petroleum products more than tripled, from around 11 million metric tons to more than 36 million metric tons. Combined with increased world market prices for petroleum, oil export earnings shot up from $1 billion in 1977 to $6.7 billion in 1985, accounting for about a third of incremental exports over the same period (Lardy 1992a, 696).

Exports of manufactured goods rose considerably during the 1980s (table 2.2). However, their share of total exports changed little because of increased exports of oil and, to a lesser extent, increased agricultural

Table 2.2 Manufactured exports, 1980–93

Year	Billions of dollars	Percent of total exports
1980	9,009	49.2
1981	11,757	53.3
1982	12,260	55.1
1983	12,616	56.6
1984	14,219	54.3
1985	13,540	49.5
1986	19,672	63.8
1987	26,217	66.4
1988	33,126	69.7
1989	37,468	71.3
1990	46,177	74.4
1991	55,700	77.5
1992	67,949	79.9
1993	75,090	81.8
Memo items:		
Rates of growth (percent per year)		
1980–85		8.5
1985–93		23.9
1980–93		17.7

Sources: Ministry of Foreign Economic Relations and Trade, *Almanac of China's Foreign Economic Relations and Trade*, 1993, 479; *China Economic News* 15, no. 7 (21 February 1994).

exports following the dramatic resurgence in agricultural production in the late 1970s and early 1980s. In short, the growth of manufactured exports just matched the 8.5 percent rate of growth of total exports in the first half of the decade. Thus in the first half of the 1980s, there was little evidence of the emergence of comparative advantage as a factor influencing the composition of China's exports. The growing exports of petroleum were particularly inappropriate because economic growth was constrained by domestic energy shortages (Lardy 1992b, 88–91).

However, as China's domestic market reform strategy, discussed in the previous chapter, took hold after the mid-1980s, the commodity composition of China's exports was transformed. In particular, the price reforms, combined with steps toward the adoption of a somewhat less overvalued domestic currency, led to a shift away from the reliance on petroleum exports toward the export of products in which China enjoyed a comparative advantage. Exports of crude oil and refined petroleum products declined steadily from their peak level of 1985, both in absolute amount and particularly as a share of total exports (Lardy 1992a, 696). On the other hand, the share of manufactured goods in China's total exports rose from half in 1985 to more than four-fifths by 1993. As shown in table 2.2, manufactured goods exports increased by an average annual rate of almost 24 percent during this period. Much of this increase was accounted for by increased exports of labor-intensive manufactures such as textiles, apparel, footwear, and toys and sporting goods. The share of China's total exports accounted for by these four categories grew from 29.6 percent in 1985 to 40.2 percent in 1990. Proportionately the greatest gains came in the two categories of toys and sporting goods and footwear, both of which trebled their share of China's exports between 1985 and 1990 (World Bank 1993a, 5–9).

Equally significant in explaining the rising share of manufactured exports was the surge in exports of electrical equipment. Its share expanded from 2 percent in 1985 to 11 percent in 1990. Most of this growth was due to expanding exports of telecommunications equipment, such as black and white televisions, radio receivers, telephone equipment, and domestic electrical equipment, such as washing machines, air conditioners, and refrigerators (World Bank 1993a, 5–9).

As a result of these changes, China's exports have become increasingly labor-intensive. Textiles, apparel, footwear, and toys are among China's most labor-intensive manufacturing sectors (Lardy 1992a, 700). Exports of telecommunications equipment and domestic electrical equipment, which might appear to be more capital-intensive, are based overwhelmingly on processing and assembly-type activity. Thus they too are labor-intensive since imported components account for about four-fifths of the value of exports (World Bank 1993a, 11–12).

Although less dramatic, the commodity composition of imports also changed over the first decade or so of reform. Most notably, the share of primary commodities in total imports fell from a little over a third in 1980 to about a seventh by 1993. In large measure, this was because imports of food and live animals in 1992 increased only slightly from the level of 1980 while total imports had quadrupled. To a significant degree, this reflects the rapid expansion of domestic agricultural output in response to the higher prices and increased marketing opportunities that China's domestic reforms generated.

The share of industrial products in total imports rose from 65 to 86 percent between 1980 and 1993. This was due largely to sharply rising imports of machinery and transportation equipment, embodying higher levels of technology than could be produced domestically.

Overall, the changes in the commodity composition of both exports and imports described above moved China's pattern of trade to one much more congruent with the country's underlying comparative advantage than had been the case in the prereform era. Most of the credit is due to reforms that led to increasing market determination of domestic prices and the increased competition in the handling of trade transactions. These developments were described more fully in chapter 1.

Direction of Trade

Among socialist countries, China was among the earliest to reorient its trade patterns away from planned trade with other socialist states toward trade with market economies. In the 1950s China was linked tightly in its trade with the Soviet Union and to a lesser degree the states of Eastern Europe. During the first five-year plan (1953–57) more than three-quarters of China's imports were from these states, and they in turn absorbed more than two-thirds of China's exports (Eckstein 1966, 98).

After the decisive split with the Soviet Union in 1960, China began to fundamentally reorient its pattern of trade. However, this was not immediately apparent for two reasons. First, in the aftermath of the disastrous Great Leap Forward of 1958–60, the Chinese economy plunged into a great depression in which real economic output fell by a third. Foreign trade also plummeted (table 1.1), reaching a low in 1962, when trade was only 60 percent of the peak level achieved in 1959. Consequently, China's share of world trade also fell by more than half, from 1.9 to 0.9 percent.

Second, despite the Sino-Soviet rift, China continued to export to the Soviet Union as a means of repaying credits that had been extended to China in the 1950s when machinery and equipment imported from the Soviet Union formed the core of China's ambitious industrialization drive. A significant portion of these capital goods were acquired with credits extended by the Soviet Union. Throughout 1961–65, China maintained a significant surplus in its trade balance with the Soviet Union in order to amortize its accumulated debt. Thus the share of Chinese exports flowing to the Soviet Union fell gradually from 50 percent in 1959 to 3.5 percent in 1965. Once the debts had been cleared, exports to the Soviet Union fell further, reaching less than half of 1 percent by 1970 (*Chinese Statistical Yearbook 1981*, State Statistical Bureau, 353–59).

China's trade with Eastern European countries, with one significant exception, also shrank dramatically in the 1960s. China deliberately boosted its trade with Romania, which was attempting to break out of the Soviet orbit. By 1970 China's trade turnover with Romania was more than 10 times the level of 1962, whereas bilateral trade with the Soviet Union was less than a tenth of the 1962 level. As a result of the declining trade with the Soviet Union and almost all of Eastern Europe, on the eve of initiating its economic reforms China's trade was already over-whelmingly with market economies.

China's economic reforms did lead to further changes in the direction of China's trade. Most importantly, the role of Hong Kong increased exponentially. From the late 1970s through the mid-1980s, Hong Kong regularly purchased just under a quarter of all China's exports. However, as the commodity composition of Chinese exports shifted away from products such as petroleum—a relatively homogeneous product sold on standard international commodity markets—to more differentiated, labor-intensive manufactured goods sold on diverse consumer markets, the role of Hong Kong expanded. By the early 1990s, the share of Chinese exports going to Hong Kong had doubled compared with the mid-1980s. As will be discussed in chapter 4, most of these goods were subsequently reexported by Hong Kong firms to other countries.

In part, Hong Kong's role in marketing Chinese goods expanded because a growing share of Chinese exports were produced by joint-venture firms in South China in which Hong Kong firms had invested heavily (discussed further in chapter 3). But in part it was because Hong Kong firms had a comparative advantage in international marketing compared with either Chinese foreign trade companies, which traditionally had marketed most Chinese goods on international markets, or compared with Chinese manufacturers, which increasingly were gaining the right to sell their goods directly on international markets but lacked the experience necessary to do so efficiently. Thus the entrepôt role of Hong Kong expanded as Hong Kong merchants and trading companies de facto became responsible for the worldwide marketing of a growing share of Chinese goods (Sung 1991b).

A second significant change in the direction of Chinese trade, in addition to Hong Kong becoming more important as a distributor of Chinese goods, was the growing role of the United States as the ultimate destination for Chinese exports. The US share rose dramatically from a few percent of total Chinese exports in 1978 to 30 percent by 1992. In absolute terms, US imports from China rose from around $300 million to almost $26 billion (table 4.1).

This increase was a consequence of several factors. First, the United States is the largest economy in the world. Second, it is relatively open. As domestic reforms increased the incentives for Chinese firms to export, it was inevitable that the share ultimately going to the United States would increase. In this respect, China is no different from many other successful developing countries around the globe in recent decades. In virtually every case, the share of their exports absorbed by the United States increased significantly as their own domestic economies took off.

Moreover, China's exports increasingly were labor-intensive manufactures for which demand in the US market is relatively price-elastic.

As China increasingly exploited its comparative advantage in these products, Chinese goods displaced those provided by traditional suppliers to the US market. As a result, China's exports to the United States boomed.

The large increase in Chinese sales of labor-intensive manufactures in the United States, and to a lesser extent in Europe, led to increasing trade frictions between China and its developed-country trade partners. In the United States, the first antidumping case against a Chinese product was filed well before the signing of the bilateral trade agreement between the two countries in 1980. As bilateral trade expanded rapidly after China received most-favored nation (MFN) status, American producers who felt that Chinese imports were being sold at less than fair-market value filed numerous antidumping cases, and those who believed the imports threatened serious injury to the competing US industry filed market disruption actions. Countervailing duties or other sanctions were imposed on Chinese imports in the US market in only a few cases, and thus the application of US trade laws against China appears to have had only a modest effect on overall levels of trade. However, these cases have had a very substantial effect on specific sectors, in some cases all but eliminating trade. Moreover, the mere threat of antidumping actions, which as applied to imports from China are widely regarded as unpredictable, arbitrary, and unfair, has a broader disruptive effect on bilateral trade (Palmeter 1989).

Trade Balance

In the first few years of the 1990s, critics of Chinese trade policies frequently charged that China was pursuing a mercantilist strategy—engaging in various types of export promotion while restricting access to its own domestic market. This view was particularly common in the United States because of the growing deficits that the United States incurred in its trade with China (Harding 1992, 311 and 338). By 1991 the US trade deficit with China was $12.7 billion, second only to that with Japan, leading some to believe that China's domestic market was closed. While the bilateral trade issues will be explored in detail in the next chapter, it is important to establish the overall context in this more general chapter on China's role in the world trading system.

Two important points emerge from an examination of the data on China's trade in table 2.1. First, in two out of three years since reform began, China has run a deficit in its trade account. Moreover, over the period as a whole, China has run a large cumulative deficit. This makes China distinctly different from Japan, which has racked up continuous large surpluses since 1981 (Bergsten and Noland 1993, 31). In most years, China's balance on current account was slightly more favorable than the merchandise account, since China usually incurred a small surplus on services and had positive net transfers, which consisted largely of remittances by overseas Chinese. However, service income and net transfers were far from sufficient to offset the merchandise deficit China ran in most years. Thus, on average, China has sustained a current account deficit financed by inflows of foreign capital. The latter are discussed in detail in chapter 3. Suffice it to point out here that China's cumulative foreign debt by the end of 1992 was approaching $70 billion. Again, this is in marked contrast with Japan, which has been a large net lender to the rest of the world every year since 1980 and which since 1985 has been the world's largest cumulative creditor nation as well (Bergsten and Noland 1993, 1–2).

Second, China's trade balance moves cyclically, tracking trends in the domestic economy with a lag of only a few quarters. Its balance also has become increasingly sensitive to trends in the real exchange rate. At the very outset of the reforms, booming economic growth led to a trade deficit for several years. The central government put the brakes on economic growth in 1980 and the first half of 1981 and introduced an internal exchange rate that significantly increased the cost of foreign exchange for some importers (Lardy 1992b, 66–74). As a result, the economy slowed, and import demand fell relative to export growth. The result was a balance of imports and exports in 1981 and then a trade surplus in 1982. From that point, economic growth accelerated and the real exchange rate appreciated as the internal rate remained fixed for several years, despite price inflation that was significantly above the world rate. The trade balance consequently deteriorated to an all-time record deficit in 1985. In the second half of 1985 and throughout 1986, the government pursued a contractionary monetary policy, the growth of the economy moderated, and the deficit shrank in 1986 and 1987. Economic growth accelerated again in 1987 and 1988, leading to rising inflation and a widening trade deficit. However, a domestic economic austerity program initiated in the second half of 1988, combined with major devaluations of the currency in December 1988 and again in November 1989, slowed the growth of imports. Combined with several other measures that encouraged exports, the trade balance underwent an astonishing shift to a record surplus in 1990.

In the early 1990s, as domestic growth accelerated, the surplus eroded, and in 1993 China recorded a trade deficit in excess of $12 billion, its second largest ever. In early 1994 the State Information Center, a unit of the State Planning Commission, forecast that the deficit would fall by a third to $8 billion in 1994. The methodology underlying the forecast is not known, but it appears to reflect two factors. First, the unification of the exchange rate at the higher secondary market rate will increase the cost of foreign exchange by a factor of almost half for the one-fifth of imports that had been financed at the official rate in recent years, presumably reducing the demand for imports to less than what it otherwise would be.[1] The unification, effectively a devaluation of the *renminbi*, also will increase the incentives for exporting. Second, the government hopes to bring down the rate of economic growth, from 13 percent in 1993 to about 9 percent in 1994. That presumably will contribute to a reduction in the rate of growth of imports.

Thus the trade balances of Japan and China have evolved quite differently. Japan's global trade surplus has risen almost continuously, from $2.1 billion in 1980 to $137 billion in 1992 (Bergsten and Noland 1993, 31). China's global trade balance has moved cyclically. Imports and exports appear to respond to underlying economic macroeconomic variables and changes in the real value of the currency rather than in response to direct government administrative controls. Moreover, cumulatively since reform began, China has imported substantially more than it has exported. Since mercantilism is generally associated with national policies to attain persistent trade surpluses, the term does not describe China very well.

Predicting China's Future Trade

In the 1980s and the early 1990s, China's trade expanded more than twice as rapidly as world trade (figure 2.1). This is the fundamental reason China has entered the ranks of the world's top 10 exporters and its share of world trade is dramatically increasing. One must ask not whether this supercharged performance can continue, but when it will end. One factor explaining China's recent trade growth is its recovery from an artificially depressed initial level when reform began. But as already shown, in 1993 China surpassed the previous peak share of world trade that it had enjoyed in 1927–29 (table 1.1). What are the constraints on further expansion?

Predicting future trade expansion is complex and surrounded with uncertainties, both with regard to the future of the international trading system and the future direction of China's ongoing economic reforms. If China continues to enjoy MFN tariff status in the United States and there is no serious retrogression toward a more protectionist international trading system, I believe that over the medium term the pace of China's trade expansion will depend primarily on the growth of Chinese exports. That is because I do not believe the growth of China's imports is likely to be either significantly higher or lower than the growth of its

---

1. Prior to the unification of the exchange rate, exporters had been able to convert about four-fifths of all foreign exchange earnings to *renminbi* either directly through the secondary market or at the rate determined on the secondary market. The central government used the remaining one-fifth of foreign exchange, which it required exporters to surrender at the official exchange rate, to finance high-priority imports.

Figure 2.1 Growth of Chinese and world exports

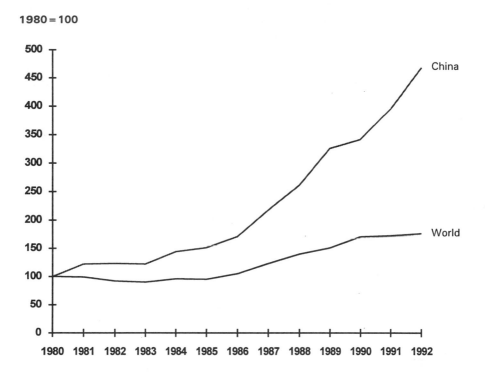

1980 = 100

Source: General Agreement on Tariffs and Trade, International Trade, various years.

exports. For example, many heavily indebted Latin American countries had to scale back the growth of their imports relative to exports after the sharp increase in the price of oil in 1973–74 in an attempt to generate export surpluses to repay their external debts. As a result, their trade growth diminished significantly compared with earlier years. Although China already has a large foreign debt, it is not likely to need to scale back imports in order to generate a trade surplus to service its debt. In 1992 China's debt service absorbed only about 10 percent of exports. Indeed, China is more likely to increase its external borrowing in order to run the modest annual trade deficits that were characteristic of most of the 1980s (table 2.1). Thus I do not share the view that China is likely to return to a persistent balance of trade surplus as economic growth declines from the unsustainably high rates experienced in the first half of 1993 (Lawrence Summers, statement before the Senate Committee on Banking, Housing, and Urban Affairs, Subcommittee on International Finance and Monetary Policy, 25 May 1993, 4).

On the other hand, China's borrowing would have to grow exponentially to allow imports to grow significantly faster than exports over any sustained period. And this seems most unlikely in light of China's relatively conservative past borrowing practices.

Analytically, in predicting the growth of exports one must look at both supply and demand factors—that is, both the ability of China to increase production for world markets and the ability of these markets to absorb more Chinese goods. To anticipate, this analysis suggests that China will become an even more important trading country as the turn of the century approaches. However, the rate of China's trade expansion will probably begin to converge with the rate of growth of world trade by the late 1990s if not sooner.

On the supply side, one must begin by pointing out that the high Chinese foreign-trade participation rates sometimes cited by both Western and Chinese writers are quite misleading. For example, Yang Deming (1992, 11), a researcher at the Economic Research Center of the State Planning Commission, writing in the main public journal of the Ministry of Foreign Economic Relations and Trade, reported that in 1991 the ratio of foreign trade to GNP in China had reached the astonishing level of 39.1 percent, with the ratio for exports alone standing at 19.4 percent. He went on to compare China with the United States, Japan, Germany, and India, pointing out that the ratio of exports to GNP in China was several times that of the United States and India and more than twice as high as Japan's. Although Yang acknowledged that China's GNP was somewhat undervalued in these calculations, he concluded that China's trade dependence was "very high" by the standards of large, advanced Western countries. The implication clearly is that there is very little room left for China to expand its participation in the international economy.

However, these high participation ratios result from using the official exchange rate to measure Chinese output in dollars, the denominator in the trade or export ratio calculation. Since, as already suggested in chapter 1, this procedure understates the real output of the Chinese economy by a factor of about three, the trade ratio conversely is overstated by the same factor. After making the appropriate adjustments, the ratio of exports to GNP in China is below that of all of the comparator countries cited by Yang. In short, I do not believe that, by comparison with other large countries, China is in any sense already trading "too much."

Thus, the growth of exports will continue to depend largely on the domestic macroeconomic cycle and the trade policy regime of the Chinese government. For example, in 1993 the growth of exports declined dramatically to only 8 percent, just half the pace of expansion sustained since 1978. This was due in part to an extraordinary 13 percent rate of growth of real GNP. The effect of sharply higher domestic demand, which pulled in more imports, was reinforced by exchange rate policy.

Although the price level rose about 20 percent, the official exchange rate changed little, and, as will be discussed in greater detail in chapter 4, for most of the first half of 1993 the central government imposed a price ceiling on the price of foreign exchange on the swap market. As a result, the value of the domestic currency rose much of the year, further undermining the incentive to export.

On the demand side, one must begin by recalling that the commodity composition of Chinese exports has shifted decisively toward manufactured goods over the past 10 years. Further, China has demonstrated an ability to move up-market, exporting higher quality, higher valued-added products over time. Demand for these products in world markets is relatively income-elastic, meaning that China can anticipate growing sales as the world economy expands.

Moreover, China's starting point in terms of sales of manufactured goods in developed-country markets was relatively modest. In 1988, developing countries as a group supplied only 3 percent of all manufactured goods consumed in OECD countries. China supplied only one-tenth of this, or three-tenths of 1 percent. If OECD consumption of manufactures continued to grow at 4 percent, the same rate as that of the previous decade, while Chinese exports and other developing-country exports continued to grow at 15 percent and 14 percent, respectively, China's share of OECD consumption of manufactured goods would rise to only four-tenths of 1 percent by 1998. And developing countries as a group, including China, would be the source of less than 5 percent of OECD consumption of manufactured goods. This relatively modest hypothetical increase in China's share of manufactured goods consumption does not suggest that developed-country markets are so saturated that a further sizable trade expansion into the late 1990s would not be economically feasible if China were capable of sustaining a 15 percent rate of growth of exports (World Bank 1993a, 143–44).

The same relatively optimistic conclusion is supported by an examination of the price consequences of the dramatic expansion of China's exports in the 1980s and early 1990s. Those who question the ability of developing countries to promote their domestic growth through greater reliance on international trade frequently suggest that a rapid expansion of trade depresses the prices developing countries receive for their exports relative to the prices they pay for their imports. China provides an interesting test of this proposition, since its role as a trading nation expanded more rapidly than any other country in the 1980s.

The data in table 2.3 show China did suffer a secular deterioration in its terms of trade in the 1980s and the early 1990s. The prices China received for its export goods fell by 20 percent relative to the prices that it paid for its imports. However, that was entirely due to rising prices paid for imports. Prices received for exports actually rose, albeit modestly. Since China's exports are more concentrated than its imports, as a

Table 2.3 Terms of trade, 1980–92 (1987=100)

Year	Export price index	Import price index	Terms of trade
1980	107	88	122
1985	95	78	122
1987	100	100	100
1990	112	112	100
1991	111	113	98
1992	114	117	97

Source: World Bank (1993d, 111).

first approximation we may assume that China is a price taker for imports. That is, an increase in Chinese imports of a broad range of commodities such as industrial machinery and equipment, transportation equipment, and chemical fertilizers is unlikely to change world prices. Actually, this is not strictly true, since in 1992–93 changing levels of Chinese imports of commodities such as gold, steel, copper, nickel, and zinc did exert a noticeable effect on the prices of these goods in world markets. On the other hand, Chinese exports are increasingly concentrated in labor-intensive manufactures. For several of these commodities, China's share of world exports has grown so dramatically that it could have lowered prices significantly. For example, the share of world exports of travel goods and handbags supplied by China rose from 12.3 percent in 1985 to 30.6 percent by 1990. Similarly, China's share of world exports of toys rose from 6.5 percent to 22.3 percent, of clothing from 8.0 to 14.4 percent, of footwear from 2.4 to 13.3 percent (World Bank 1993a, 161). Yet despite the large increases in the absolute level and in the share of China's exports of these and other products in world exports, the index of prices China received for its exports actually rose somewhat. This is all the more remarkable since the price of petroleum, which accounted for 10 percent of China's exports in 1987, the base year for the data in table 2.3, fell by 45 percent between 1980 and 1992.

Thus, China's gains from increasing participation in the international division of labor in the 1980s and early 1990s do not appear to have been eroded by price increases normally attributable to increasing export volumes. Thus, there is no obvious basis for arguing that a further expansion of its trade would lead to an adverse movement in China's terms of trade.

While this aggregate analysis suggests that developed-country markets should be able to accommodate substantially greater quantities of Chinese exports and that the prices China would receive for higher volumes of exports would not necessarily deteriorate, a more disaggregated analysis does raise some questions about whether this will in fact be the case. These questions arise, in the first instance, because Chinese products face unusually high tariff and nontariff barriers in OECD markets. Clothing, footwear, and textile yarns and fibers, which together account for one-quarter of China's exports, face tariffs in OECD markets that are very much higher than the average tariff rate of 4.8 percent. The European Union's tariffs on clothing and footwear average 20 and 23 percent, respectively. Australian tariffs on these products are even higher, 49 and 43 percent, respectively (World Bank 1993a, 146). Given the evolving structure of Chinese exports discussed earlier in this chapter, one would anticipate that it will become more difficult, not less, for China to achieve the same rate of growth of exports as in the 1980s and early 1990s. Put another way, China's overall export growth of more than 13 percent per annum in 1980–93 was achieved in large measure by the rapid expansion—almost 18 percent annually through 1993—in manufactured goods exports. And this in turn is explained by the even more rapid growth of labor-intensive manufactures such as clothing, textiles, footwear, and toys. Thus, the average tariff faced by Chinese exports has been rising, even though the tariff structure in the importing countries has been unchanged in recent years.

In addition to facing relatively high tariffs, China's exports, particularly its manufactures, are subject to relatively severe nontariff barriers in developed-country markets. Table 2.4 summarizes the coverage of nontariff barriers placed on China's total exports and on manufactures specifically, in three major markets in 1990: the United States, the European Community, and Japan. The United States is the most restrictive, with nontariff barriers such as quotas on almost half of all imports from China and more than three-fifths of manufactured goods imports. The new bilateral textile agreement that took effect in 1994 is emblematic. It allows no increase at all in imports of Chinese garments and textiles in 1994 and restricts the increase to 1 percent annually in each of the next two years. Moreover, its coverage extends to silk garments. By comparison, under the previous agreement the annual increase allowed was 4.4 percent, and silk garments were not subject to any restrictions at all. Since textiles and apparel have accounted for almost one-fourth of US imports from China in recent years, the new agreement can be expected to have a significant effect on bilateral trade.

Japan is clearly the least restrictive, primarily because it does not subject Chinese clothing and textile imports to quota restrictions under the Multi-Fiber Arrangement (MFA), as do the United States and the countries of the European Union.

In the United States, the protection nontariff barriers provide is substantial—in most cases exceeding what the protection tariffs afford. For most products, total effective protection ranges from 40 to 80 percent (World Bank 1993a, 148–50). Again, the implication is that it may be

Table 2.4 US, EC, Japan: share of imports from China covered by nontariff barriers,[a] 1990 (percentages)

	United States	European Community	Japan
All goods	47	30	22
Manufactures	62	48	27

a. Numbers are the percent of imports from China subject to "hard-core" nontariff barriers, including import prohibitions, quantitative restrictions, variable import levies, MFA restrictions, nonautomatic licensing, and countervailing and antidumping measures.

Source: World Bank (1993a, 148).

increasingly difficult for China to maintain the growth of manufactured exports and thus overall exports that it did in the 1980s and early 1990s, particularly between 1985 and 1993.

Looking at specific products also raises questions. European actions in recent years have restricted imports of Chinese products ranging from textiles and bicycles to televisions and videotapes. In early 1994 the European Union imposed quotas on seven additional items—gloves, toys, footwear, porcelain kitchen and tableware, ceramic kitchen and tableware, and radios. The 1994 quotas were set at levels as much as 21.5 percent below actual 1992 imports. These actions suggest China will be subject to more adverse trade actions as import penetration levels rise.

This more disaggregated analysis suggests that China is somewhat vulnerable to increasing protectionism in developed-country markets. Thus China's trading future depends not only on the maintenance of its MFN status in the United States, but also very much on the future evolution of the world trading system.

Not only would China be a major beneficiary of the maintenance of an open world trading system, China's trade may receive a major boost from the successful completion of the Uruguay Round of trade talks. A recent World Bank study (1993a, 150–51) suggests that, under Uruguay Round trade liberalization, Chinese exports to the United States, the European Union, and Japan would increase by almost 40 percent, more than twice the 15 percent increase expected for all developing-country exports to the same developed-country markets.

China's benefits from tariff reductions and other reforms contained in the Uruguay Round agreement, particularly from the 10–year phaseout of the MFA, are substantially greater than those likely to accrue to other developing countries for two reasons. First, as already noted, most of China's exports are manufactured goods. These face higher tariff protection in developed-country markets than the raw materials and primary products that dominate the exports of many developing countries. Second, Uruguay Round tariff reductions would erode the margins of the special preferences, not available to China, that many other developing countries enjoy. Examples are Generalized System of Preferences (GSP) status in the US market and Lomé Convention and special regional preferences in the European Union.

However, it is important to note that the Bank's estimate of the gains to China from the conclusion of the Uruguay Round presumed that the United States would apply the GATT to China. It is more likely, however, that the United States will invoke Article 35, the so-called nonapplication provision, when China becomes a participant in the GATT. As is explained in chapter 3, the provisions of the Jackson-Vanik amendment to the Trade Act of 1974 preclude granting China permanent MFN status in the US market. Since one of the most important provisions of the GATT is the requirement that all contracting parties grant each other permanent MFN trading status, the United States will almost certainly invoke Article 35, allowing it to opt out of applying all or part of the GATT to China.

Thus, it is far from certain that China will benefit from either the anticipated tariff reductions or the phaseout of MFA quotas in the United States. A separately negotiated bilateral agreement will spell out which portions of the GATT, including the MFA phaseout, the United States will apply to China.

The conclusion of this analysis of the demand side is that the evolution of the world trading system increasingly will become the most important factor determining the growth of Chinese exports. Much of the expansion of China's trade in the 1980s was a recovery from artificially depressed levels of the past. As import penetration levels for a growing number of products reach certain threshold levels, protectionist responses in developed-country markets could constrain future growth. The nonapplication of the GATT, particularly the MFA phaseout with respect to China by the United States, might even lead to an erosion of China's sales in the US market and a subsequent increase from producers in other countries who will provide the products previously supplied by China.

China and the GATT

China and Taiwan are the two most significant trading nations that are not contracting parties to the General Agreement on Tariffs and Trade, the world's most important international trade organization. China formally applied to become a contracting party to the GATT in July 1986. Formal negotiations to pave the way for China's participation in the GATT have been under way since the first meeting of the Working Party for China in February 1988. Yet there is no apparent end in sight. The chronology in the appendix identifies the key events.

Perhaps no accession process has been as complex and as time-consuming as China's. Ironically, China was one of 23 original signatories to the GATT in 1948. However, the Nationalist government withdrew from the GATT in 1950. The problems surrounding China's participation are both political and economic.

On the economic side, the major question is how to accommodate a socialist state, even one as reformed as China's, in a body that was essentially established to promote trade among market economies. The contradiction arises because one key principle of the GATT is that contracting parties regulate trade through tariffs rather than direct controls such as quotas, licenses, and other administrative instruments. This requires that there be a direct link between international and domestic prices. Otherwise a negotiated tariff reduction might be meaningless—for example, if the initial price in the nonmarket economy had been set administratively at a level substantially above that prevailing in world markets.

As already mentioned in chapter 1, this problem was finessed in the accessions of both Poland and Romania because they became contracting parties, not on the basis of any economic reforms they had undertaken, but rather on a pledge to increase their imports from other contracting parties. The Chinese foreclosed this option. From the beginning they indicated that they expected to participate in the GATT on the basis of reductions in their tariff levels.

One potential method of dealing with the residual nonmarket character of the Chinese economy is for the existing contracting parties to include what is referred to as a selective safeguard clause in the protocol governing China's participation in the GATT. Under Article 19 of the GATT charter, countries that experience such a large increase in imports of a particular product that its own domestic production suffers serious injury would be allowed to adopt emergency restrictions on imports if such a clause is included in the accession protocol. These restrictions may include increased customs tariffs or increased nontariff barriers. Reserving the right to increase tariffs or implement nontariff barriers on imports on a selective basis—that is, on imports coming from a single country—is a serious qualification to the principle of nondiscrimination. However, the US position for several years has been that China must accept such a provision in the protocol governing its participation. By 1992, largely in response to a burgeoning deficit in its trade with China, the European Community was making it increasingly clear that it held a similar position.

Other economic issues are also at stake. Among them is China's expectation that it will be regarded by the GATT as a developing country. That would allow China to continue to provide significant tariff protection for so-called infant industries. Some indications are that China expects to protect automobiles, machinery and electronics, chemicals, and perhaps aviation. Developing countries in the GATT are allowed to maintain existing tariff levels and licensing requirements for an initial three-year period. Thereafter, extensions must be negotiated. However, the Chinese clearly hope that in some cases they will be able to avoid a complete phaseout of all protection for up to 10 years.

The political problems related to China's participation are even more complex. First, China insists that it has requested resumption of its seat in the GATT rather than accession. At first glance this might seem to be a somewhat arcane distinction, but it goes to the heart of the issue of Taiwan's status. The present government of China does not wish to imply that it accepts that the withdrawal from the GATT in 1950 was legal since that, in turn, might imply that it recognized the validity of Taiwan's claim to sovereignty over all of China. China's position is that under international law the formal establishment of the People's Republic of China on 1 October 1949 represented the replacement of Nationalist Party rule by Communist Party rule of the mainland. Thus, China maintains that Taiwan's withdrawal from the GATT in 1950 was illegal and did not represent the wishes of all of China.

China now hopes that other states will allow it to resume its participation in the GATT, thus implicitly accepting the Chinese position on the withdrawal. This poses profound difficulties for the GATT because when Taiwan withdrew, it did so in accordance with GATT regulations, and its withdrawal was accepted by the GATT, notwithstanding the claim that China made at the time to all international organizations that ''it was the sole lawful representative of China'' (Herzstein 1986, 403–04).

China's desire that other countries accept its view that China's status as a founding signatory to the GATT was not affected by the withdrawal of Taiwan in 1950 creates further complications. If China did not really withdraw from the GATT in 1950, what was its status until 1986, when it requested to resume its participation? China's view is that it had suspended its GATT activities as a founding signatory.

But if China was a contracting party to the GATT that had merely ''suspended its GATT activities,'' shouldn't China be asked to pay past annual dues as a condition for resuming its participation? No, says the Chinese government, under the principle of ''nonretroactivity.'' Its position is that this principle should be embedded in the protocol setting forth the conditions for China's resumption of its status as a contracting party, thus relieving it from any obligation to pay 35 years of cumulative dues.

The second political problem surrounding China's accession is that China is determined that Taiwan will not accede to the GATT before China and that China will sponsor Taiwan's accession. Taiwan's January 1990 application was to participate in the GATT as ''The Customs Territory of Taiwan, Penghu, Kinmen and Matsu'' (the latter three are small islands lying between Taiwan and China that have been under Taiwan's administration since 1949). Taiwan seeks to participate in the GATT under Article 33, which allows territories with autonomy in customs matters to have separate representation (Jacobson and Oksenberg 1990, 102). This differs from the accession of Hong Kong and Macao in 1986 under Article 26.

Since Hong Kong acceded to the GATT in 1986, prior to China's resumption of sovereignty in 1997, one might ask on what grounds China can object to Taiwan's accession preceding its own. The Chinese position is that it agreed to the separate participation of Hong Kong in the 1984 Joint Declaration of the Government of the United Kingdom and the Government of China. And the GATT agreed that Hong Kong could maintain its separate status after 1997. The Chinese government maintains that it has not agreed to the accession of Taiwan and that this should not occur until after it resumes its own status as a contracting party.

Third, China seeks unconditional MFN treatment from all contracting parties. Yet under the 1974 Jackson-Vanik amendment to the Trade Act of 1974, US law precludes granting MFN status in the US market to nonmarket countries that restrict emigration. Although China has enjoyed continuous MFN status in the US market since 1979, this is possible only because the law provides that if the president is satisfied that a country is not restricting emigration he can request, in a report to the Congress, a waiver of the amendment.

In sum, China is clearly already one of the world's major trading countries, and for decades it has traded largely with market economies. Based on the projections in this chapter, China's trade is likely to continue to grow at rates well above the expansion of world trade, although precisely how much is likely to be influenced by the degree of protectionism China encounters in developed-country markets, particularly the United States.

Although China seeks to protect broad sectors of its domestic economy from international competition, the evolution of China's global trade and current account since reform began clearly does not support the contention that China is a mercantilist trading country. The best prospect for reducing further the protection that China provides to various domestic industries is likely to be the document that spells out the terms under which other countries are prepared to have China participate in the GATT. Further specific suggestions for attaining this objective are spelled out in chapter 5.

3

Participation in International Capital Markets

China has emerged as a major participant in international capital markets. As reflected in the data in table 3.1, China's total external debt grew steadily in the 1980s and the early 1990s, reaching about $69 billion at the end of 1992. In 1992 China's total external indebtedness exceeded that of India for the first time, making China the second largest debtor nation among low- and middle-income developing countries. Only Indonesia is more indebted. But China's exports in 1992 were two and a half and more than three times larger than those of Indonesia and India, respectively. Thus China's debt-service ratio is significantly lower than these countries', indicating that higher debt levels will not necessarily pose a problem for China or its lenders.

The structure of China's debt is relatively favorable. At the end of 1991, only one-fifth was short term, a significantly smaller share than in the mid-1980s, when short-term debt comprised from one-third to as much as a half of total debt. One-third of China's long-term debt is official. These funds are either multilateral in origin, as in the case of loans from the World Bank or the Asian Development Bank, or bilateral, as in the case of loans from the Japanese Overseas Economic Cooperation Fund or other national development agencies. The interest rates the Chinese pay on such loans are generally quite low and the term of the loans fairly long so that the grant component is quite high. For example, in the late 1980s and early 1990s the grant component of Japanese official development assistance ranged from two-thirds to four-fifths. In the most favorable case—funds from the World Bank's soft loan window,

Table 3.1 External debt, 1978–92

Year	Millions of dollars	Year	Millions of dollars
1978	623	1986	23,746
1979	2,183	1987	35,296
1980	4,504	1988	42,362
1981	5,797	1989	44,812
1982	8,358	1990	52,554
1983	9,609	1991	60,851
1984	12,082	1992	69,321
1985	16,722		

Source: World Bank (1993e, vol. 2, 90).

the International Development Association (IDA)—the initial commitment fee has been waived on all loans in recent years, no interest is levied on the loan, the repayment of principal is waived for the first 10 years, and the term of these loans extends three decades. The result is that the loan is essentially a gift. At year-end 1991, one-fifth of China's official borrowing was from the IDA.

Borrowing from International Organizations

China's entry into the World Bank and the International Monetary Fund in 1980 paved the way for China's borrowing from them. However, China's initial borrowing was quite modest. In 1980–81 China was in a phase of economic retrenchment, cutting back on investment projects, including some of those that would have been financed with funds borrowed from the World Bank. After the executive directors approved an initial loan for $200 million in June 1981, only a single loan agreement for $60 million was reached in fiscal 1982. Lending increased to $600 million in 1983 and then reached $1 billion for the first time in 1984 (table 3.2). Annual loan commitments grew steadily, and at mid-year 1989 cumulative loans by the Bank totaled $7.4 billion, of which $3.2 billion had already been disbursed (Jacobson and Oksenberg 1990, 109–21 and 155). At that time, loans extended to China made up 7.1 percent of the Bank's regular loan portfolio and 14.4 percent of total IDA loans outstanding.

The Tiananmen massacre of students resulted in a decisive reduction in World Bank lending to China. The Bank continued to disburse funds on previously committed loans, and as a result actual disbursements were almost unchanged in fiscal 1990, the 12-month period following Tiananmen, compared with fiscal 1989. However, new loan commitments collapsed (table 3.2).

Table 3.2 IBRD and IDA loans to China, 1981–93[a] (millions of dollars)

Fiscal year	Commitments			Disbursements		
	Total	IBRD	IDA	Total	IBRD	IDA
1981	200	100	100	0	0	0
1982	60	0	60	1	0	1
1983	614	463	150	71	4	67
1984	1,040	616	424	197	73	124
1985	1,102	660	442	566	354	212
1986	1,137	687	450	606	324	282
1987	1,424	867	556	705	306	399
1988	1,694	1,054	640	1,110	553	557
1989	1,348	833	515	1,090	604	486
1990	590	0	590	1,086	591	495
1991	1,579	602	978	1,267	668	599
1992	2,526	1,578	949	1,331	553	778
1993	3,172	2,155	1,017	1,575	812	763
Cumulative through 1993	16,485	9,614	6,871			

a. The World Bank's fiscal year ends June 30. Data on disbursements are gross—they do not reflect repayments. Totals may differ from the sum of individual items shown because of rounding.
Sources: World Bank, *Annual Report*, various years; *World Development Report 1993* (table 5.1).

In 1990, however, lending on new projects resumed, largely because the United States in January announced it would no longer oppose all lending to China. Initially the Bank's executive directors considered only new loans that were directed toward meeting basic human needs. This policy reflected a compromise between countries that favored harsher sanctions and those that felt that the Bank, by suspending approval of any new loans for several months, had already held China to a higher standard than had prevailed in the past. In fiscal 1990, the first full year after Tiananmen, only $590 million for five new projects was approved. At least four of the projects—for increasing agricultural productivity and raising farmers out of subsistence in Jiangxi and Hebei Provinces, for reconstruction following an earthquake in Shanxi and Hebei Provinces, and for national afforestation—met the poverty alleviation criterion mentioned above or an environmental protection criterion that subsequently was added.

Eventually the scope of approved loans expanded further as the United States, the only major industrial country still imposing economic sanctions on China, assumed a lower profile and allowed its executive director to abstain rather than vote against loans for broader economic development. Thus by December 1990 the Bank resumed lending for industrial and transportation infrastructure projects. These included road construction, urban development, and industrial development projects.

As a result, the Bank's lending almost tripled in fiscal 1991. In 1992 new loan commitments exceeded the previous peak of fiscal 1988, and China emerged as the number-one borrower from the World Bank, displacing India, which had been the largest borrower for about two decades. This position was maintained in 1993, when new IBRD and IDA lending to China hit a new peak of $3.172 billion.

This surge in World Bank lending raised new issues for China's borrowing. Traditionally the Bank has limited its annual lending to any single country to no more than 12 percent of its regular (non-IDA) loan portfolio. The limit has been exceeded, however, when the Bank's executive board decided to exceed it. For example, beginning in 1984 and continuing for several years, India received from 13 to 15 percent of annual IBRD lending. By 1992 China was approaching this limit, and in 1993 lending to China absorbed 12.7 percent of regular IBRD loans. It remains to be seen whether the Bank will continue to approve projects for China that absorb such a large share of annual new lending.

Moreover, China's access to IDA funds from July 1993 through June 1996 will be scaled back. In fiscal 1993 China absorbed more than 15 percent of all IDA lending. Although the Bank expects to lend up to $22 billion between fiscal 1994 and 1996, the Bank has decided to give greater weight to creditworthiness as a criterion in the allocation of loans. Since China enjoys considerable access to international credit markets and as Moody's Investors Service in the fall of 1993 raised its rating on Chinese sovereign debt, the mix of loans from the Bank beginning in fiscal 1994 will likely contain a smaller share of more concessional IDA lending and a larger share of regular IBRD loans. Within a few years, IDA lending to China probably will be phased out completely.

In addition to borrowing regular and IDA funds, China also benefits from the activities of the International Finance Corporation (IFC), a member of the World Bank Group that promotes private enterprise in developing countries. Through the end of the third quarter of 1993, the IFC had undertaken eight projects in China. The total commitment of funds was a little over $100 million, of which about four-fifths was loans and one-fifth was equity financing. The IFC opened an office in Beijing (separate from the existing IBRD resident mission) in the fall of 1992 in anticipation of an increase in its activities in China.

China has also borrowed, although more modestly, from the Asian Development Bank (ADB). China became a member of the ADB in March 1986 and began to borrow in 1987. As shown in table 3.3, the

Table 3.3 Asian Development Bank's lending to China, 1987–93 (millions of dollars)

Fiscal year[a]	Commitments	Disbursements
1987	133.30	0.0
1988	282.90	2.71
1989	39.70	52.03
1990	50.00	55.44
1991	496.30	172.72
1992	903.00	178.54
1993[b]	1,050.00	

a. The ADB fiscal year ends 31 December.

b. The figure for 1993 is projected based on loan commitments of $860 million through early November and the anticipated approval of two additional projects prior to the end of the year.

Source: Asian Development Bank, *Annual Report*, various years.

ADB's new lending commitments to China rose initially but then collapsed in 1989 and 1990, as sanctions were imposed in the wake of Tiananmen. ADB disbursements, however, continued to rise during the sanction period, as China implemented projects financed with previously committed loans. Also, as in the case of the World Bank, new lending volumes grew significantly after the moratorium on new loans was lifted in late 1990. In 1993 China was the third largest borrower from the ADB, after Indonesia and India. By the end of 1993, the Bank had approved 30 projects with a cumulative loan value of almost $3 billion.

Cumulative Chinese borrowing from the ADB is much less than that from the World Bank for perhaps four reasons. First, China has been borrowing from the ADB for a shorter period; its entry into the ADB in 1986 was well after its entry into the World Bank in 1980.

Second, the overall lending of the latter is substantially greater than that of the ADB. For example, in 1990 the World Bank's lending commitments for new projects, inclusive of IDA funds, were almost $21 billion, more than five times the $4.0 billion in new lending commitments of the ADB, inclusive of loans by the Asian Development Fund (ADF).

Third, China, like India, has never been ruled eligible for loans from the ADB's soft loan window, the ADF. Like the IDA, ADF lending has a high implicit grant component and is available only to the poorest member countries. Neither China nor India was a member of the ADB when the plans were made for the country-by-country allocation of the fourth replenishment of the ADF, covering 1987–90. The ADB had originally hoped for an expansion of the ADF to $10 billion in the fifth replenishment, covering 1992–95, which would have allowed the inclusion of both China and India. But commitments for the ADF replenishment from developed countries fell far short, and in December 1991 the funding level was fixed at only $4.2 billion. As a result of this disappointment, the Bank added neither China nor India to the eligibility list. Indonesia, Pakistan, Bangladesh, and the Philippines, in that order, currently are, and are likely to remain, the largest borrowers from the ADF.

Finally, since China's borrowing is restricted to loans financed from the Bank's ordinary capital resources, ADB borrowing may be less attractive than some alternatives. Although ordinary ADB loans have relatively long maturities of 10 to 30 years and grace periods of two to seven years, the interest rate on them approaches commercial rates. Thus, the implicit grant component of the ADB's regular loans is relatively modest, making them less attractive to the Chinese than funds available through several other sources, such as IDA or official bilateral lending from developed countries.

China also receives technical and other forms of assistance from a variety of United Nations agencies, such as the World Health Organization, UNICEF, and the World Food Program. The latter, for example, initiated activities in China in 1979 and has provided over $700 million in food assistance for 55 development projects. UNICEF activities began in 1980. By the end of 1993, China had received $160 million in assistance for a broad range of projects. UNICEF has earmarked over $50 million for projects in China in its 1994–95 fiscal year. Some activities of UN agencies are coordinated through the United Nations Development Programme (UNDP). By the late 1980s, China was the largest single recipient of UNDP funds.

National Development Assistance

China receives official development assistance in the form of low-interest, long-term concessionary loans from virtually every industrialized country. The flow of official bilateral development assistance began modestly, averaging a few hundred million dollars annually in 1979–81 (table 3.4). Bilateral loans exceeded the half-billion dollar level in 1982 and the billion-dollar level in 1988.

On the eve of Tiananmen in May 1989, the total value of commitments made under these programs was reported to be $19.9 billion. Commitments from Japan alone stood at $10.6 billion. Agreements covering projects valued at $12 billion had actually been signed, and disbursed loans under these agreements stood at $5.2 billion ("Key Projects Receive Foreign Aid," *China Daily*, 1 May 1989).

After economic sanctions were imposed by most Western nations on China in 1989, commitments of new development assistance were suspended for periods of one to two years (table 3.4, column 2). There was a

Table 3.4 Official bilateral borrowing, 1979–92
(millions of dollars)

Year	Actual	Commitments
1979–81	925.09	
1982	553.07	2,435.20[a]
1983	715.72	901.78
1984	722.98	504.65
1985	486.32	1,020.53
1986	841.30	1,443.52
1987	797.98	2,018.94
1988	1,179.21	3,356.89
1989	2,149.02	1,471.25
1990	2,523.57	719.37
1991	1,809.85	2,243.25
1992	2,566.38	4,389.72

a. For 1979–82.

Source: Ministry of Foreign Economic Relations and Trade, *Almanac of China's Foreign Economic Relations and Trade,* various years.

drop of more than half in commitments of bilateral concessionary lending in 1989, and virtually all these commitments were made in the first half of the year. Although some new commitments—for example, by the French government—were made beginning in the latter part of 1990, the total value of new loan commitments that year was again down by more than half compared with the previous year and was probably at the lowest level of the 1980s. Since 1990, however, new official bilateral aid commitments to China have increased dramatically, reaching a record high of almost $4.4 billion in 1992.

Fluctuations in the magnitude of official bilateral aid funds actually used were smaller than the fluctuations in commitments. This was because many countries, notably Japan, continued to disburse funds under agreements previously signed even as they imposed a moratorium on new commitments. As a result, bilateral loans disbursed in 1989 were almost double those of 1988. The level of disbursements rose again in 1990 but by less than a fifth. However, foreign concessionary loans actually used fell by more than a third in 1991, reflecting with a lag the sharp reduction in new loan commitments in 1989 and 1990. In 1992 the level of disbursements rose significantly, surpassing the previous peak level of 1990, again reflecting with a lag the higher commitments evident after 1990.

Because Japan was the first country to offer a program of official bilateral assistance to China and because Japan is far and away the largest source of bilateral lending to China, its assistance is worth examining in some detail. Japan's assistance to China flows through several channels: Japan's official bilateral development agency, the Japanese Overseas Economic Cooperation Fund (OECF); the Japanese Export-Import Bank; the Japanese International Cooperation Agency; and others.

Of these, OECF is the single most important source of funds. As table 3.5a shows, Japan has extended three major OECF assistance packages with loans totaling more than ¥1.6 trillion ($10.0 billion). These packages are extended periodically, usually on the occasion of a visit to China by a Japanese prime minister. The loan funds are then disbursed annually, as the Japanese agree to finance specific projects proposed by the Chinese. For example, the first round of credits, worth ¥330 billion ($1.4 billion), was extended by Prime Minister Masayoshi Ohira in December 1979, and subsequently projects were approved annually to finance port and railway construction. The second package of ¥470 billion ($2.1 billion) was offered by Prime Minister Yasuhiro Nakasone during his trip to China in March 1984. The third, for a record ¥810 billion ($6.5 billion), was offered on Prime Minister Noboru Takeshita's visit to China in August 1988. The third loan package emphasized infrastructure and transport projects as well as chemical fertilizer plants to support Chinese agriculture.

As previously mentioned, commitments for new projects within this third package were suspended after June 1989 but then resumed in November 1990. By the end of fiscal 1990, three groups of projects were approved with funding totaling ¥120 billion ($80 million). In fiscal 1991 the Chinese proposed a package of 14 new Japanese-assisted projects totaling ¥554.5 billion ($4.1 billion). The projects included thermal and hydroelectric projects, rail, road, subway, and port construction projects, chemical fertilizer plants, and urban water supply systems. Most but not all were approved by the Japanese.

In August 1993 the fourth individual loan agreement within the six-year package was signed. It provided ¥138.7 billion ($1.3 billion) in funding for a broad range of infrastructure projects including port and airport development, water supply systems, hydropower and thermal power projects, telecommunications systems, and chemical fertilizer plants.

Cumulatively the Japanese OECF by the end of 1993 had signed loans for specific projects totaling ¥528.2 billion (about $5 billion), roughly three-fourths of the total loans to be extended to China during 1990–95.

The resulting annual flow of funds through 1991 is shown in table 3.5b, under the ODA loans column. Disbursements of official development assistance loans provided through the OECF rose steadily throughout the 1980s, reaching a peak in 1989 and then falling in 1990

Table 3.5a   Japan: bilateral economic assistance to China, 1979–95

OECF package	Fiscal years[a]	Billions of yen	Billions of dollars[b]
1	1979–83	330	1.4
2	1984–89	470	2.1
3	1990–95	810	6.5

Table 3.5b   Japan: annual bilateral disbursements, 1979–91 (millions of dollars)

Year	Total	ODA loans	Grants	Export credits
1979	2.6	0.0	2.6	0.0
1980	407.6	0.9	3.4	403.3
1981	27.7	15.6	12.1	0.0
1982	368.8	330.2	38.6	0.0
1983	561.0	299.1	51.1	210.8
1984	531.2	347.9	41.5	141.8
1985	442.5	345.2	42.7	54.6
1986	889.4	410.1	86.9	392.4
1987	866.0	422.8	130.3	312.9
1988	1,144.1	519.9	154.7	469.5
1989	1,650.2	669.2	164.1	816.8
1990	1,705.9	538.5	201.3	966.1
1991	872.1	423.7	194.1	254.4

OECF=Overseas Economic Cooperation Fund

ODA=official development assistance

a. The Japanese fiscal year ends 31 March.

b. Dollar values in table 3.5a are calculated using the exchange rate prevailing at the time each of the packages was announced.

Source: Organization for Economic Cooperation and Development, Geographical Distribution of Financial Flows to Developing Countries, various years.

and 1991 in response to the suspension of new project loan approvals after the Tiananmen massacre in June 1989.

What the table does not show is the extent to which Japan has dominated ODA to China and the relative importance of China as a recipient of Japanese ODA. Throughout the 1980s, Japan on average supplied more than three-fourths of all the official development loans the Chinese received. The Japanese share of grants to China was slightly less, but as discussed below, Japan continuously has been far and away the single largest source of grant funds as well.

Of equal interest is the relative importance Japan assigned to China in its overall ODA program. Japan was among the very first countries to initiate an ODA program for China in 1979, with a modest $2.6 million in grants. Its ODA loan program began at a low level in 1980, when China ranked only 21st among the recipients of Japanese bilateral development assistance, absorbing less than a half a percent of Japan's ODA. But in the early 1980s, China's share of Japanese ODA loans rose sharply to more than 5 percent, and from 1982 through 1986 China was the largest recipient of Japanese ODA loans. Starting in 1987, it was the second largest recipient after Indonesia.

In addition to official development assistance, among developed countries the Japanese also provide the largest flow of official export credits to China. Indeed, in most years the credits provided through the Japanese Eximbank exceed the total volume of official export credits provided by all other developed countries combined. For example, from 1988 through 1990 the Japanese Eximbank alone was responsible for more than three-quarters of all official export credits. The second largest supplier was Canada, which supplied only 10 percent. The United States ranked a distant third with only 7 percent of total official export credits. Since the grant component of these loans is less than 25 percent, they are not counted as part of official development assistance by the OECD. But since the terms of the loans are more favorable than commercial borrowing, they have been an important element in financing Chinese imports.

Finally, Japan has been the largest source of grant funds, not only exceeding those provided by any single country but also those provided by all multilateral sources combined (table 3.5b). Grant aid, which imposes no obligation of repayment, has been used for such projects as the 1,000–bed Sino-Japanese Friendship Hospital constructed in Beijing in the early 1980s.

Commercial Borrowing and Securities Sales

China's entry into the World Bank and the International Monetary Fund in 1980 paved the way for not only concessionary loans, discussed above, but also commercial borrowing. China borrows on international capital markets via both syndicated loans and the sale of bonds and stocks.

Trends in commercial borrowing and the use of commercial trade credits are reflected in table 3.6. Annual commercial borrowing reached a peak of almost $2.6 billion in 1987 and then declined over the next three years for two reasons. First, in the latter part of 1988, as China instituted an austerity program to curtail accelerating inflation, foreign borrowing was cut back. That trend was reinforced after 4 June 1989,

Table 3.6 Bank borrowing, 1979–92 (millions of dollars)

Year	Commercial borrowing	Trade credit
1979–81	6,699.60	206.52
1982	860.40	188.51
1983	0.45	105.64
1984	122.27	133.26
1985	526.49	126.48
1986	1,494.89	177.61
1987	2,579.62	472.90
1988	2,434.73	888.22
1989	2,269.43	641.80
1990	2,043.96	898.43
1991	2,442.52	1,161.97
1992	1,778.32	989.11

Source: Ministry of Foreign Economic Relations and Trade, *Almanac of China's Foreign Economic Relations and Trade,* various years.

when most foreign banks discontinued making new loan commitments. As the retrenchment policy was abandoned and the rate of investment accelerated in the early 1990s, foreign borrowing increased somewhat. But even through 1992, levels of commercial borrowing remained below the peak of 1987. In part, this presumably reflects the increasing flows of foreign investment and concessionary bilateral official borrowing.

Export credits provided by the Japanese and other export-import banks or similar institutions rose sharply after the mid-1980s before falling in 1989 in response to Western sanctions imposed after Tiananmen (table 3.6). But new record levels were attained in 1991–92, with export credits averaging about a billion dollars annually.

In addition to commercial borrowing and export credits, China also has gained access to increasing quantities of foreign exchange through the sale of bonds on international markets. China's first international bond issue was a private placement of a ¥10 billion issue of the China International Trust and Investment Company (CITIC) in January 1982 in Tokyo. The second private placement, of a ¥5 billion issue also in Tokyo, was by the Fujian Investment and Enterprise Corporation in August 1983. In 1984 the Bank of China issued ¥20 billion in bonds through a public offering, also in Japan.

After this rather slow start, the pace accelerated dramatically. The number of issues increased, the average amount in each issue increased, and markets beyond Tokyo were tested. In 1985 nine issues were sold, all through public offerings. These included two issues on the Frankfurt market denominated in marks and one in Hong Kong denominated in Hong Kong dollars.

Through the end of 1988, a total of 39 bond issues, valued at $4.25 billion, had been sold on international markets. Tokyo remained the most important market, where 21 issues were floated, but China also sold bonds in Singapore, Luxembourg, and London as well as returning to the Frankfurt and Hong Kong markets. The number of institutions issuing bonds rose to seven, including the Guangdong, Tianjin, and Shanghai International Trust and Investment Corporations, the Bank of Communications, and the Ministry of Finance (Igarashi 1989).

The violence of Tiananmen temporarily ended China's access to international bond markets. Moody's Investors Service and Japanese bond rating agencies downgraded and placed a credit watch, respectively, on Chinese bonds. A ¥15 billion issue by the Guangdong International Trust and Investment Corporation scheduled for June 1989 in Tokyo was canceled. China did not reenter international bond markets until mid-1991, when the Bank of China floated a ¥20 billion issue in Tokyo.

Although reentry into the Eurobond market was delayed, once it began there was a virtual flood of new issues.[1] The Bank of Communications, the Bank of China, and the People's Construction Bank separately issued Eurobonds with a total value of $370 million in the second half of 1992. CITIC issued $150 million in bonds in April 1993, followed in May by the Guangdong International Trust and Investment Corporation and the Bank of China with issues totaling $250 million. In June both the Construction Bank and the Bank of China returned to the market with Eurobonds totaling $320 million. China Investment Bank and the Hainan International Trust and Investment Company issued Eurobonds totaling $180 million in August.

A record occurred in July 1993, when CITIC sold $250 million in bonds in New York. That was the first US bond issue, a so-called Yankee bond, by any mainland Chinese institution since the Communist Party came to power in 1949. The People's Construction Bank followed CITIC's lead, signing an agreement in early September to float its first bond issue of $120 million in the US market.

In September 1993 the Ministry of Finance returned to the market for the first time since 1987 with a ¥30 billion ($283 million) offering. In value terms that was the single largest post-Tiananmen issue on the Euromarket by any Chinese entity. The five-year bonds were priced to yield 4.375 percent. The spread over the yield on Japanese government bonds of comparable maturity was a remarkably small 75 to 85 basis points, suggesting that investors demanded only a modest risk premium.

---

1. For a comprehensive listing of China's international bond issues from the beginning of 1992 through October 1993, see World Bank (1993e, vol. 1, 123–24).

In part, the modest risk premium reflected an upgrading by Moody's Investors Service of China's sovereign debt from Baa-1 to single-A-3. That upgrading, in September 1993, restored the rating Moody's had assigned to China's sovereign debt prior to the downgrading that occurred in the wake of Tiananmen. Although Baa-1 debt is considered investment grade, it is in the lower range of that spectrum. Since some European fund managers aren't allowed to purchase bonds rated lower than single-A-3, the upgrading probably resulted in a lower interest rate on the Chinese Ministry of Finance's Eurobond issue in September 1993.

Buoyed by that success, the ministry in mid-October floated a $300 million issue of 10–year bonds in Asia. That was the first Asian government entry in what has become known as the Dragon bond market. These issues are usually denominated in US dollars and listed only in Asian markets outside Japan. In early October, Guangdong Investment Limited issued $102 million in bonds. In early 1994 new records were set. The Ministry of Finance sold $1 billion of 10-year global Eurobonds, the largest issue ever by any Chinese institution. The Bank of China planned a $500 million Yankee bond issue in late February, its largest ever on any market and the largest ever Chinese Yankee bond issue as well.

Several points emerge from the record since China's reentry into the market in mid-1991. First, the volume of bond sales has increased significantly compared with the pre-Tiananmen period. Projecting for the last quarter of 1993, the World Bank estimated that Chinese entities issued bonds worth about $2.7 billion in international markets in 1993, bringing the total issues in 1992–93 to $3.8 billion. On an annual basis that is three times as much as was being sold between China's first international bond issue in 1982 and the end of 1988.

The increase in the volume of bond issues has made China a significant participant in the international bond market for the first time. The World Bank's figures and projections ranked China in 1992 and 1993 seventh and eighth largest among developing-country issuers of international bonds (World Bank 1993e, vol. 1, 22).

Second, the average issue is much larger. In the pre-Tiananmen period, issues of ¥5 billion and ¥10 billion were common, and the largest dollar-denominated issue was $200 million. Since 1991 yen-denominated issues as low as ¥10 billion or ¥15 billion have been rare, and the largest dollar-denominated issue was $1 billion, five times the largest pre-Tiananmen issue.

Third, the Japanese domination of the market has ended. In the pre-Tiananmen period, most bonds were denominated in yen and issued in Japan. The lead underwriters of these issues were almost invariably large Japanese firms such as Nomura, Sanwa, Daiwa, and Yamaichi. Japanese firms sometimes were the lead managers, even for issues floated in Luxembourg and Singapore. In the early 1990s, most issues were denominated in dollars and sold on the Eurobond market or in the United States. Although Nomura was the lead underwriter for the offering of the Chinese Ministry of Finance in the dragon bond market, CS First Boston, Morgan Stanley, Merrill Lynch International Limited, Lehman Brothers Asia, Salomon Brothers, and others all were active underwriters.

Finally, the terms under which China's bonds are being sold suggest that any risk premium associated with Tiananmen has evaporated. Even bond issues by provincial investment companies, which are not sovereign entities and do not carry a Bank of China or other central government guarantee, have generally been sold on quite favorable terms.

In addition to the sale of bonds, China is also raising investment funds through the sale of equities to foreigners on both domestic and international markets. Since 1992 the Chinese have raised funds by selling for hard-currency B shares in a selected number of companies listed on its two domestic stock exchanges: Shanghai and Shenzhen.

Sales of equities on international markets have been made by both Chinese domestic firms and by Chinese-controlled foreign corporations. In the former category, China Brilliance Automotive, a Bermuda-based holding company that controls Jinbei Automobile Company in Shenyang in Northeast China, was the first Chinese company listed on the New York Stock Exchange in the fall of 1992.[2] In July 1993 China Tire, a multifirm company put together by the Hong Kong–based financier Oei Hong Leong, was listed on the New York Stock Exchange. Other NYSE-listed China companies include the Shanghai Petrochemical Co. Ltd. and the EK Chor Motorcycle Company of Shanghai. US underwriters have a large number of other Chinese enterprises, including some major industrial companies, they are preparing to list.

For Chinese companies unable or unwilling to meet the marginally higher disclosure requirements of the New York Stock Exchange, the Hong Kong Stock Exchange beckons. In October 1992 the Chinese authorities approved a plan to list nine companies on the Hong Kong market. By the end of 1993, six had been brought to the market, including one of China's largest industrial companies, the Shanghai Petrochemical Company. The Chinese Securities Regulatory Commission has approved a second batch of 22 Chinese companies for listing on foreign markets in 1994. Most are expected to be listed on the Hong Kong market. But several will be listed in New York, and one or two may achieve a listing in London.

Chinese-controlled foreign corporations have also raised funds by selling shares abroad. One prominent example is Citic Pacific Ltd. It

---

2. For a comprehensive listing of China's 1992 international equity issues, both public and private placements, see World Bank (1993e, vol. 1, 133).

Table 3.7 Inward foreign direct investment, 1979–93 (millions of dollars)

Year	Contracted	Actual
1979–82 (cumulative)	6,999	1,767
1983	1,917	916
1984	2,875	1,419
1985	6,333	1,959
1986	3,330	2,244
1987	4,319	2,647
1988	6,191	3,739
1989	6,294	3,773
1990	6,987	3,755
1991	12,422	4,666
1992	58,736	11,292
1993	110,850	25,750
1979–93 (cumulative)	220,630	60,210

Sources: Chinese Statistical Abstract 1993, State Statistical Bureau; *Wall Street Journal*, 2 February 1994, A13.

issued HK$7.3 billion ($950 million) in new shares in early 1993. Citic Pacific Ltd., which is listed on the Hong Kong Stock Exchange, is 49 percent owned by Citic Hong Kong, a foreign subsidiary of the Beijing-based China International Trust and Investment Company (CITIC).

Foreign Direct Investment

Foreign direct investment flows into China have grown almost continuously since China's economic reforms began in the late 1970s (table 3.7). Despite the fact that China has been a major borrower from the World Bank for years, foreign investment always has been more important as a source of foreign capital for China. Moreover, by 1992 and continuing in 1993, foreign investment expanded to become by far the single most important source of external capital for China, surpassing the combination of bilateral development assistance and borrowing commercially and from international organizations.

Foreign investment began modestly after the passage of a joint venture law in 1979 and the establishment of special economic zones on China's southeast coast in 1980. Foreign funds that were actually used averaged only a few hundred million dollars annually in the first few years China was open to foreign investment and did not exceed a billion dollars until 1984 (table 3.7). Foreign investment that was actually used rose steadily for several years afterward. In the wake of Tiananmen, the growth of foreign investment in China came to a halt, although many observers were surprised when the actual inflows remained on a plateau of about $3.7 billion annually rather than falling precipitously.

As foreign investors' consternation over Tiananmen waned in the early 1990s, direct investment surged to new high levels, exceeding $4.5 billion in 1991, $11 billion in 1992, and then almost $26 billion in 1993. There is little doubt that some of these recorded inflows reflect Chinese capital that had first flown out and then returned to China to take advantage of the tax incentives provided to foreign-invested firms. However, overlooking this impossible-to-measure factor, China not only attracted more foreign investment in 1992 than any other developing country, it was the recipient of almost one-fourth of the total flow of foreign direct investment to developing countries (World Bank 1993e, vol. 1, 51). With actual investment exceeding $25 billion in 1993, China remained far and away the largest developing-country recipient of foreign direct investment and absorbed an even larger share of the total flow of foreign direct investment to developing countries.[3]

The cumulative total of foreign direct investment actually undertaken in China through 1993 exceeded $60 billion. The cumulative value of foreign investment contracts signed was almost four times as large, exceeding $220 billion.

The ten largest foreign-funded enterprises in 1992, ranked by sales, are shown in table 3.8.

The explanation for the long-term rise in foreign direct investment in the 1980s and the surge in the early 1990s is not obvious. China had a limited legal structure, meaning property rights were not well-defined; its currency was not convertible, meaning that would-be investors had

---

3. Data on actual and approved foreign direct investment used in this study are those compiled and published by the Chinese government. The former almost certainly overstate the magnitude of FDI, and the degree of overstatement appears to have increased in recent years as controls on capital outflows have weakened. The overstatement arises largely because foreign-invested enterprises enjoy tax and other advantages not available to Chinese firms. Foreign exchange that flows out of China, by both legal and illegal means, frequently returns disguised as foreign investment. In addition to this bias, it is not clear whether the annual data on actually utilized foreign investment includes reinvested profits and deducts repatriated earnings of existing foreign-invested firms, as is the standard international practice.

Data on approved foreign investment are even less reliable because the Chinese appear to include the value of all contracts signed for foreign invested enterprises. Sometimes, these contracts are not approved at higher levels of the Chinese government; not infrequently the approved investment project envisioned in the contract is never undertaken, and in ventures that are implemented, the actual amount of FDI may fall far short of the contractually specified amount. For these reasons, analysis in this study is based primarily on data on actual foreign investment. Data on approved foreign investment probably are a good indicator of the direction of future actual FDI.

Table 3.8 Leading foreign-invested firms in China, 1992[a]
(thousands of yuan except where noted)

Firm	Sales volume	Pretax profit	Assets	Foreign exchange income (thousands of dollars)
Shanghai Volkswagen AG	7,108,000	715,100	2,314,760	23,390
Beijing Jeep Corp., Ltd.	3,489,890	261,830	2,089,000	8,210
Guangzhou Peugeot Automobile Co., Ltd.	2,444,380	187,450	1,550,900	16,000
Nanhai Oil Industry Co., Ltd.	1,446,820	none	454,970	none
Huaqiang Sanyo Electronics Co., Ltd.	1,402,710	23,750	507,150	149,400
Shanghai Bell Telephone Equipment Co., Ltd.	1,317,730	343,550	1,193,220	3,490
Shenyang Jinbei Bus Manufacturing Co., Ltd.	1,290,270	none	821,210	none
Guangzhou Iron and Steel Co., Ltd.	1,267,950	86,550	740,170	9,980
Shenzhen Konka Electronics (Group) Co., Ltd.	1,212,790	100,780	549,800	105,000
Shenzhen Zhonghua Bicycles (Group) Co., Ltd.	1,165,920	127,460	1,643,320	268,420

a. Companies are ranked according to their annual sales volume in 1992.

Source: "China's Biggest 500 FFEs (Productive) in 1992," *China Economic News*, Supplement No. 13, 13 December 1993.

to plan on exporting part of their product to have an assured source of hard-currency earnings; and growing corruption made the investment environment increasingly inhospitable, particularly for American multinationals. China overcame these negative factors because it liberalized its foreign investment regime almost continuously, its economy was among the fastest growing in the world, and its economic ties with South Korea and Taiwan, which were highly constrained in the early years of reform, became increasingly important over time.

The initial foreign investment law contained many provisions that potential foreign investors regarded as onerous. It limited access of joint ventures to the Chinese domestic market, made no provision for wholly foreign-owned companies, required that the chairman of each joint venture be Chinese rather than a foreign national, and put a finite life on all joint ventures, after which ownership had to revert to the Chinese part-ner. However, over time the Chinese systematically eased these restric-tions (Pearson 1991, 70–78). In 1986 the state promulgated a new law on wholly foreign-owned enterprises. The practical effect of this law was enhanced when implementation regulations were promulgated in 1988. Similarly, in the spring of 1990 an amendment to the 1979 joint venture law eased the initial limit on the duration of joint ventures.

In 1985 China formally opened secondary markets for foreign exchange. Initially operating in only a handful of cities, these markets quickly spread, and the transaction volume rose remarkably. By 1989 trade turnover involving foreign-invested firms exceeded $2.3 billion. Foreign sellers of foreign exchange, taking advantage of the more favor-able price they could receive in the market compared with exchanges through the Bank of China at the official exchange rate, actually out-numbered buyers (Lardy 1992b, 60–61). Thus foreigners were net sellers of foreign exchange. But the increased flexibility provided by the swap market meant that direct investments intended to produce primarily for the domestic market became increasingly attractive.

In the early 1990s China was developing what was rapidly becoming one of the most liberal foreign investment environments in the develop-ing world. Although the largest existing ventures in 1992 were almost all in manufacturing (table 3.8), the Chinese successively opened up other sectors of the economy to foreign investment.

Retailing

Foreign investment in retailing was highly restricted prior to 1992. But in the second half of 1992, substantial liberalization began. The new regula-tions allow Sino-foreign joint ventures in retailing of most but not all products, generally with a 50-50 split in equity shares, in Beijing, Shang-hai, Tianjin, Guangzhou, Dalian, Qingdao, and the five special eco-nomic zones. These joint ventures receive the right to import directly commodities they sell, rather than going through an established state trading company, but imports are not supposed to comprise more than 30 percent of retail sales.

Despite these restrictions, the change stimulated a huge influx of foreign investment in shopping complexes by major retailers, such as Japan's Yaohan, as well as highly publicized individual stores such as those of Nike and Giordano in Shanghai, Benetton and Baskin-Robbins in Beijing, American Place opened by the former chairman of R. H. Macy in Guangzhou, and Seibu in Shenzhen.

By the end of 1993, agreements had been signed for eight large shop-ping centers in China. The first to open was the Beijing Lufthansa Youyi Shopping City, a Sino-German joint venture with a total investment of $10.4 million. A second, much larger 200,000 square meter Dong'an

Shopping Arcade in the Wangfujing section of the capital is expected to open in 1995. The total investment in this project, backed by Sun Hung Kai Property in Hong Kong, is said to be $300 million. But by far the most ambitious plans announced to date are those of Yaohan. It was among the first of the large international retailers to open joint venture department stores in China. But its largest project, in which it has roughly a third ownership, is a gigantic 21-story, 144,000 square meter complex under construction in Shanghai. When it opens in 1995, it will be the largest store in Asia.

Chinese officials have openly discussed expanding the scope of foreign investment to include wholesale trade as well, but no formal announcement has yet been made. Yaohan, however, has already announced plans to establish its own wholesale distribution system to serve its department stores in Shanghai and Beijing and a planned chain of hundreds of supermarkets as well.

Power Generation

In 1992 the Chinese authorities opened the electric power generation sector to foreign investment. Before, major multinational companies only sold power generation systems to China. Since liberalizing the investment regime in this sector, the Chinese have been encouraging build-operate-transfer (BOT) projects. Under these schemes, foreign firms finance a power generation project, build the facility, and operate it for a fixed period before ownership reverts to the Chinese partner in the venture. The forerunners of this policy change were the 700-megawatt Shajiao B power plant near Shenzhen in Guangdong Province, built and operated by Hong Kong's Hopewell Holdings, and the Daya Bay nuclear power station near Hong Kong. Shajiao B was completed in 1987, and a second project, Shajiao C, is under construction. The Daya Bay nuclear plant, one-quarter owned by China Light and Power in Hong Kong, is the biggest foreign-invested power plant in China. It was expected to start operation in November 1993 with 70 percent of the output to be sold in Hong Kong.

By mid-1993, 53 joint Sino-foreign projects in thermal, hydro, and nuclear power generation and in power transmission had been concluded. Many are located in Guangdong, the Pudong development area in Shanghai, and in Shandong Province—areas that are taking the lead in decontrolling electric power prices and, in some cases, even considering guaranteeing a specified rate of return on foreign investment. Since state-fixed prices have long been very substantially subsidized, this decontrol is a prerequisite for foreign investment in the power sector. One example of a project that would guarantee a fixed rate of return is a proposed $2.5 billion joint venture in Shandong involving China Light and Power, French government-owned Electricité de France, and the

Shandong Provincial Electric Power Bureau. The model for pricing is similar to that between China Power and Light and the Hong Kong government, which guarantees the company a return of 15 percent on investment in fixed assets.

Transportation

Liberalization in this sector includes road, air, and rail transport. The most well-publicized venture in transport is the superhighway being built between Shenzhen and Zhuhai by Hopewell Holdings. The first phase, the link between Shenzhen and Canton, may open in early 1994. Hopewell is financing the entire cost of the road construction in exchange for a share of the tolls that will be collected in the first 30 years after opening, during which time Hopewell will operate the toll road. Hopewell expects to earn considerable additional amounts from rights it has to the development of retail and other facilities at highway interchanges

Joint ventures in air transportation are also developing rapidly. In 1992 alone, 15 joint foreign-Chinese aviation companies were approved. They included new airline companies offering passenger service on domestic routes and joint ventures for the construction and management of airports and for aircraft maintenance. Pilots and maintenance personnel are already being trained by foreign firms. The only portion of the industry not yet open to foreign participation is air traffic control. This restriction might be lifted as well since the lack of controls on the flow of aircraft currently is a greater constraint on the growth of Chinese civil aviation than are aircraft, pilot, and crew shortages.

Of the joint ventures that have been announced, the Xiamen-Swire Aircraft Engineering Co. Ltd., an aircraft maintenance company initially capitalized at about $30 million, is perhaps the most interesting. The partners are the Hong Kong Aircraft Engineering Company (HAECO) controlled by Swire Pacific Ltd., Xiamen City in Fujian Province, and a Chinese firm controlled by the Civil Aviation Administration of China. Cathay Pacific, 52 percent owned by Swire Pacific Ltd., was the first major foreign airline to indicate that it would shift some maintenance work to the joint venture. Within months of the joint venture's establishment, Japan Air Lines announced that it would purchase a 10 percent stake in the venture and that it would shift some of its Boeing 747 maintenance to the joint venture's facility in 1996, when it is anticipated it will begin operations. Subsequently, the Singapore Airline Engineering Co. Ltd. also purchased a 10 percent share of the joint venture.

Regulations also have been liberalized to allow joint ventures or even wholly foreign-owned firms to build railroads. The first large project announced is a joint venture, 251-kilometer line in Zhejiang Province between Jinhua, which lies on the main north-south rail line linking

Canton with Beijing, and Wenzhou, on the coast. The venture is capitalized at Y172 million and is 51 percent owned by a Hong Kong firm. The line, which runs through a large area in the south-central portion of the province that lacks rail service, will provide a dramatic boost for Wenzhou's port, which in the absence of any rail service has languished. Construction on the line began in December 1992, and it is expected to open to traffic in 1996.

A much larger project, still in the discussion stage, is a high-speed rail link on the 1,300-kilometer Beijing-Shanghai line, China's busiest route. The main competitors reportedly are a consortium of three German firms (Siemens, AEG, and Deutsche Waggonbau) and a group of French companies.

Port Development

China has also opened its ports to foreign direct investment. The largest and best-publicized deals involve Hong Kong International Terminals, 60 percent owned by Hutchison Whampoa of Hong Kong. In 1991 Hong Kong International Terminals signed an agreement to create a joint venture to modernize and operate Shanghai's existing container facilities and to build additional new facilities. The new joint venture, Shanghai Container Terminals, is 50 percent owned by Hong Kong International Terminals and will be run by a senior executive of the latter firm. The agreement should lead to a much-needed updating of Shanghai's container shipping facilities. If the joint venture succeeds in a tentative plan to offer shipping services as well, it may inject some competition in the Shanghai port, where two state shipping companies have a joint monopoly on all services.

Hong Kong International Terminals also has formed a joint venture with the port of Zhuhai, adjacent to Macao, to operate feeder services to Hong Kong and develop Zhuhai's deep water port. Finally, in 1993 it also became the largest shareholder in a consortium of firms purchasing control of the port facilities of Yantian in Guangdong Province, northeast of Hong Kong. The other participants in the consortium are the Chinese Ocean Shipping Company (Cosco), Mitsui, and Kumagai Gumi (Hong Kong).

Other Hong Kong companies have also announced major investments in port development. Kowloon Wharf and Godown Company has signed a joint venture with Wuhan Municipality to build a major container transshipment facility to serve central China and to develop a deep water port area in the Wuhan harbor, which is on the Yangzi River.

Oil Exploration and Exploitation

Although the Chinese opened up the South China and Bohai Seas for exploration by foreign-owned firms in the early 1980s, until recently with only a few exceptions they had held multinational oil firms at bay in the East China Sea and in the Tarim Basin in Xinjiang in Northwest China. But in May 1992 the State Council approved the opening of two large areas in the East China Sea totaling more than 70,000 square kilometers for development by multinational oil firms. Bids on these areas were submitted before a 30 June deadline. By the end of 1993, the China National Offshore Oil Corporation (CNOOC) had signed the first 10 contracts for exploration in the East China Sea. The foreign firms involved were the US companies Chevron, Exxon, Texaco, and the Maxus Energy Corporation, the Italian Agip, the Danish Maersk, Royal Dutch Shell, the Japanese Petroleum Engineering Co. Ltd., and Teikoku Oil Co. Ltd.

In the fall of 1992, only a few months after announcing the opening of the East China Sea to foreign firms, Premier Li Peng indicated that China would drop its long-standing policy of relying entirely on indigenous resources for the development of petroleum reserves in the Tarim Basin. In February 1993 China formally opened 73,000 square kilometers in the southeast corner of the Tarim Basin to foreign firms. More than 60 foreign oil firms, about one-third based in the United States, submitted bids for exploration rights by the tender closing on 31 October 1993. China awarded the first contract to a consortium led by Exxon on 20 December 1993.

In February 1993 the Chinese National Petroleum Corporation also announced the opening of 14 other blocks in onshore areas for development in cooperation with foreign oil companies. The bidding process for these sites began in January 1994 with a 31 August deadline for submitting bid documents. In late 1993 the Chinese National Petroleum Corporation announced that it was considering opening additional blocks for foreign development in areas that are considered more desirable than those opened in 1993.

Services

The People's Insurance Company of China (PICC) for decades enjoyed a monopoly in the Chinese domestic market. After many years of discussion, the American International Group (AIG), the world's largest insurance company, in 1992 received a license to sell a limited number of insurance products in Shanghai. In addition, by 1993 two Hong Kong–based joint venture insurance companies had national licenses to sell insurance products.

China also allows foreign banks to invest in selected domestic Chinese banks. The first joint venture bank, the Xiamen International Bank, was established in August 1985. Unlike foreign bank representative offices or even foreign branch banks, joint venture banks are allowed to take *renminbi* deposits, but only as an agent of the Chinese bank that is the partner in the joint venture. By mid-1993 China had six joint venture banks, three wholly foreign-owned banks, three joint venture financial companies, and one wholly foreign-owned financial company.

Ties with Taiwan and South Korea

In addition to this multifaceted liberalization of the foreign investment regime, increasingly close ties with Taiwan and South Korea also fueled increased foreign direct investment. The largest single source of foreign investment in China during most of the 1980s, accounting for about two-thirds of the total, was Hong Kong, followed by the United States and then Japan. Since the late 1980s, however, Taiwan and South Korea have become considerably more important sources of foreign direct investment. By 1991, for example, Taiwan surpassed the United States to emerge as the third largest source of foreign direct investment. In 1992 actual investment from Taiwan exceeded $1 billion, and it surpassed Japan as the second largest source of foreign direct investment.

South Korean investment is still modest but can be expected to grow in the wake of the establishment of formal diplomatic relations with China in the fall of 1992 and the subsequent signing of a bilateral investment treaty.

To some extent, the analysis in the above paragraphs is misleading since it is based on official Chinese data on actual foreign investment used. Much of the investment that is recorded as coming from Hong Kong originates elsewhere in Asia and is channeled through Hong Kong companies. Thus some of the rise in direct investment that is identified as Taiwanese may simply reflect the more relaxed cross-straits political environment that has emerged since the late 1980s. However, even with the rise in the absolute amount of investment that is identified explicitly as Taiwanese in origin, fully two-thirds of total foreign direct investment inflows in 1992 were from Hong Kong. Thus there is little doubt that the share of total capital coming from Hong Kong and Taiwan combined has been rising since the late 1980s.

Implications of Investment for China's Trade

One important reflection of China's increasingly liberalized foreign investment regime is the growing importance of exports of foreign-invested firms. As shown in table 3.9, the share of China's total exports produced in foreign-invested firms increased from only 1 percent in the mid-1980s to more than one-quarter in 1993. The implications of China's unusually high dependence on exports from foreign-invested firms will be discussed further in chapter 5.

Table 3.9 Exports of foreign-invested firms,[a] 1985–93

Year	Millions of dollars	Percent of total exports
1985	320	1.1
1986	480	1.6
1987	1,200	3.0
1988	2,460	5.2
1989	4,920	8.3
1990	7,800	12.5
1991	12,100	16.8
1992	17,400	20.4
1993	25,240	27.5

a. Exports are inclusive of those produced by equity joint ventures, contractual joint ventures, and wholly foreign-owned firms.
Sources: Lardy (1992a, 711); "China's Foreign Trade Increases to Reach $195.7 Billion," New China News Agency, People's Daily, 10 January 1994; table 2.1.

Summary

China has clearly emerged as a major participant in international capital markets in the early 1990s. China continues to make substantial advantage of borrowing opportunities from international financial organizations, such as the World Bank and the Asian Development Bank, and to enjoy substantial inflows of funds provided by official bilateral development assistance.

But by the early 1990s, foreign direct investment became the single most important source of external funding. And the flow of FDI has increasingly been supplemented with funds from the sale of bonds and equities on international markets. All indications are that these international sources of capital will be of increasing importance to China.

4

Economic Issues in US–China Relations

Economic issues moved to the fore in bilateral US-China relations in the early 1990s. The driving force was the growing US deficit in its trade with China. The deficit stimulated demands in the United States that China improve its intellectual property protection and that China liberalize access to its domestic market. Negotiations to improve the intellectual property rights regime are motivated in part by the assumption that if this environment improves, US firms would be more likely to want to sell in China, thus increasing US exports. On the other side of the equation, market access negotiations have been motivated by the assumption that under a less restrictive import regime Chinese consumers and industrial enterprises would be more likely to be able to purchase goods produced in the United States. Concern about the growing bilateral trade imbalance has also become entangled in the annual renewal of China's most-favored nation (MFN) status in the US market. These and other economic issues in the bilateral economic relationship will be analyzed in this chapter.

Bilateral Trade Balance

The United States has incurred a deficit in its trade with China every year since 1983 (table 4.1). Although initially trivial in size, the deficit grew rapidly after 1985 and was expected to be well over $20 billion in 1993. As a result, China's share of the overall US trade deficit rose rapidly. In 1989 China had the sixth largest deficit with the United States. In 1990 it recorded the third largest. Beginning in 1991 China's

Table 4.1   United States: trade with China, 1978–93 (millions of dollars)

Year	Exports[a]	Imports[b]	Balance
1978	821	324	+497
1979	1,724	592	+1,132
1980	3,754	1,058	+2,696
1981	3,603	1,865	+1,726
1982	2,912	2,284	+628
1983	2,173	2,244	−68
1984	3,004	3,065	−61
1985	3,856	3,862	−10
1986	3,106	4,771	−1,665
1987	3,497	6,293	−2,776
1988	5,021	8,511	−3,490
1989	5,775	11,990	−6,235
1990	4,806	15,237	−10,431
1991	6,278	18,969	−12,691
1992	7,418	25,728	−18,309
1993[c]	6,318	23,013	−16,695

a. US exports are valued f.a.s.
b. Imports are valued on a customs valuation basis.
c. First three quarters of the year.
Source: US Department of Commerce.

deficit became the second largest, exceeded only by that of Japan. Because the large and growing deficit underlies many other contentious issues in the bilateral relationship, it is worth examining the underlying numbers in some detail.

The US Department of Commerce data in table 4.1 are the basis for US claims about the growing bilateral trade imbalance. However, these data are subject to certain weaknesses and limitations. The principal problem arises from the increasing role of Hong Kong as an entrepôt. As already mentioned, by the early 1990s more than two-fifths of all Chinese exports were being sold in the first instance to Hong Kong. But the great majority of these goods were sold onward to other destinations, particularly the United States and Europe.

The United States and China use similar principles in the compilation of trade data. Exports are attributed to the declared country of destination for goods leaving the country, and imports are attributed to the country of origin for goods entering the country. But if both countries use the same principles to compile trade data, why do the United States and China have such different views of the bilateral trade balance—each claiming that it has a deficit in its trade with the other? For example, in 1990, while the United States claimed a deficit in its trade with China of $10.4 billion, the Chinese asserted they had a bilateral deficit of $1.7 billion.

The main reason that the figures on bilateral trade vary so greatly is the asymmetric role of Hong Kong. Put simply, Hong Kong's role is much more important in the marketing of Chinese goods in the United States than in the marketing of US goods in China. In 1990, for example, almost two-thirds of all US imports from China were goods that had been reexported from Hong Kong. By 1992 the proportion was more than 70 percent. Reexports of US goods from Hong Kong to China, however, accounted for only about a fifth and a fourth of total US exports to China in 1990 and 1992, respectively (tables 4.2a and 4.2b).

These widely varying proportions become more understandable if one examines the commodity composition of trade between the United States and China. Hong Kong companies play no role whatsoever in several of the most important US exports to China. In 1992, for example, US exports of aircraft amounted to $1.7 billion, almost one-fourth of all US exports to China. These planes are purchased or leased by Chinese companies without the participation of firms in Hong Kong. The planes are flown directly to mainland airports without passing though Hong Kong. Similarly, raw logs, another major US export to China, are shipped directly from ports in the Pacific Northwest to a variety of Chinese ports. None enter via Hong Kong, and Hong Kong firms never assume ownership of the logs.

On the other hand, Hong Kong companies play a major role in the sale of Chinese products in the United States, particularly for footwear, garments, and toys, which account for a very large share of total Chinese sales in the US market. But China, using the country of destination principle, records these exports as going to Hong Kong. Since Hong Kong firms actually take ownership of the goods, the Chinese customs authorities have no specific knowledge of the ultimate disposition of the goods, whether consumed in Hong Kong or shipped onward to other international destinations.

The consequence of this asymmetry is that Chinese data grossly understate the importance of the United States as a market for Chinese goods, and US data understate more modestly the importance of China as a market for US goods.

What difference would the adjustment to account for this problem make in an assessment of the US deficit? Fortunately, the Hong Kong government compiles data on reexports to individual countries and further cross-classifies the country of origin of Hong Kong's reexports to each individual destination country. Thus the official US data can be adjusted to derive a truer measure of the bilateral trade imbalance.

Table 4.2a United States: calculated value of US goods arriving in China as reexports from Hong Kong, 1989–93 (millions of dollars)

Year	US goods reexported by Hong Kong to China	Estimated Hong Kong margin on reexports of US goods to China	Reexports of US goods to China, net[a]
1989	1,316	162	1,154
1990	1,320	164	1,156
1991	1,712	214	1,498
1992	2,349	294	2,055
1993[b]	2,297	285	2,012

a. To be added to US data on exports to China.
b. 1993 data are for the first three quarters.

Table 4.2b Hong Kong: margin on the value of Chinese goods reexported from Hong Kong to the United States, 1989–93 (millions of dollars)

Year	Chinese goods reexported by Hong Kong to the US	Estimated Hong Kong margin on reexports of Chinese goods to the US[a]
1989	8,461	1,130
1990	10,482	1,400
1991	13,377	1,787
1992	18,386	2,456
1993[b]	15,997	2,136

a. To be deducted from the US data on imports from China.
b. 1993 data are for the first three quarters.

Table 4.2c United States: adjusted trade flows and deficit with China, 1989–93 (millions of dollars)

Year	Adjusted US exports	Adjusted US imports	Adjusted US deficit	Officially reported US deficit
1989	6,923	10,860	3,931	6,235
1990	5,962	13,837	7,875	10,431
1991	7,776	17,182	9,406	12,691
1992	9,473	23,272	13,799	18,309
1993[a]	8,330	20,877	12,547	16,695

a. 1993 data are for the first three quarters.
Sources: Sung (1991a); Hong Kong Census and Statistics Department; table 4.1.

Two uncertainties arise in this adjustment. First, the value of reexports reported by the Hong Kong government is inclusive of value added by Hong Kong firms. Goods that are merely transshipped through Hong Kong are not classified as reexports since ownership of these goods is never assumed by a Hong Kong firm. Thus, to estimate the value of US goods arriving in China as reexports from Hong Kong, the reported value of reexports needs to be reduced by the value added by Hong Kong firms. A 1988 survey made by the Hong Kong Trade Development Council concluded that the Hong Kong gross reexport margin was 16 percent on Chinese goods and 14 percent on goods from third countries. Using this estimate, Sung Yun-wing (1991a, 15.7) calculated that, net of the reexport margin, the value of US goods reexported to China in 1991 was $1,156 million. This amount needs to be added to the official US data on exports to China and thus reduces the size of the officially reported US deficit by the same amount.

A second adjustment also is required since US data on the imports of Chinese goods through Hong Kong are inclusive of the value added by Hong Kong firms. This should not be counted as part of Chinese exports. Using the same methodology, Sung Yun-wing calculated that the reexport margin earned by Hong Kong firms was $1,400 million in 1990. This amount needs to be subtracted from the official US data on imports from China, reducing the size of the officially reported US deficit by the same amount.

Table 4.2c shows that after making these two corrections the US deficit in 1990 was $7,900 million rather than the officially reported $10,400 million. Similar calculations for 1991, 1992, and the first three quarters of 1993 are also shown in the table. In 1991 and 1992, the adjusted US deficit was $9.4 billion and $13.8 billion, respectively, rather than the officially reported $12.7 billion and $18.2 billion. In the first three quarters of 1993, the adjusted US deficit was $12.5 billion rather than the officially reported $16.7 billion. Thus, since 1990 the Commerce Department data have consistently overstated the US bilateral deficit in trade with China by fully one-third.[1]

Another factor to be taken into account is the effect of international capital mobility on the trade figures. A growing portion of the goods that the United States imports from China were once made in Hong

---

1. The reversion of Hong Kong to Chinese sovereignty in 1997 will not eliminate the overstatement of the US bilateral deficit in trade with China due to the asymmetric role of Hong Kong in the two-way trade flows between China and the US. The reason is that the Sino-British joint declaration of 1984 governing the future of Hong Kong calls for Hong Kong to retain its existing economic system for 50 years beyond 1997. This means that Hong Kong will retain its own currency and will continue to participate in the GATT (see discussion in chapter 2 in the section on China and the GATT). Thus, Hong Kong will maintain a system of customs separate from that of China despite the reversion of sovereignty.

Kong or Taiwan. In response to rising local wages, Hong Kong firms in the 1980s took advantage of China's liberal foreign investment regime by shifting a growing portion of their manufacturing activities to China. By the early 1990s, virtually all of their most labor-intensive manufacturing was in China. Beginning only a few years later, an increasing number of firms in Taiwan followed a similar pattern, moving production of labor-intensive goods to China in order to remain competitive in world markets. Most of this production is carried out either in joint venture firms in China or under various types of processing contracts, discussed in chapter 5. A large share of this production is located in southern counties of Guangdong Province adjacent to Hong Kong and in Fujian Province opposite Taiwan.

The movement of labor-intensive manufacturing production to China has two implications for any analysis of bilateral trade. First, the mirror image of China's growing trade surplus with the United States is the declining deficit that the United States has incurred in its trade with Hong Kong and Taiwan. The combined US deficit with China, Taiwan, and Hong Kong, referred to as the deficit with Greater China, increased less than 10 percent between 1987 and 1992 (table 4.3). The US deficit with Hong Kong and Taiwan combined shrank about $13 billion between 1987 and 1992, in part because firms in those countries moved labor-intensive manufacturing to China. Over the same period, the US deficit in its trade with China rose $15.5 billion. Of course, in response to the currency realignments associated with the Plaza Agreement of 1985, the global US deficit in the balance of trade shrank from an all-time peak of about $170 billion in 1987 to about $96 billion in 1992. Thus, the share of the US global deficit accounted for by Greater China roughly doubled, from 15 percent to 30 percent, over this period.

Nonetheless, the growing bilateral deficit of the United States in its trade with China in part reflects the increasing concentration of Asian labor-intensive manufacturing production in China. American government officials claim the US deficit is caused by Chinese import restrictions. But a more important cause seems to be the liberalization of China's foreign investment regime that has attracted record amounts of foreign direct investment, mostly from Hong Kong and Taiwan.

Second, the Chinese quite correctly point out that a large portion of the profits from its exports accrue to foreign firms. This is because by the early 1990s about half of all of Chinese exports were processed (discussed further in chapter 5). According to one estimate, China earns only about 20 cents for every dollar's worth of goods exported under processing and assembly contracts (Sung 1991a, 15.8). The World Bank in a more recent study (1993a, 12) similarly estimated that the import content of China's processed exports was 77 percent. However, in trade data, China is credited with a full dollar of exports. This has a particularly skewing effect on bilateral trade data with advanced industrial

Table 4.3 United States: trade deficit with Greater China, 1987–92
(millions of dollars)

Year	Deficit with Greater China	Deficit with China	Deficit with Taiwan	Deficit with Hong Kong
1987	25,876	2,796	17,209	5,871
1988	20,624	3,490	12,585	4,550
1989	22,644	6,235	12,978	3,431
1990	24,411	10,431	11,175	2,805
1991	23,673	12,691	9,841	1,141
1992	28,371	18,309	9,346	716

Source: US Department of Commerce, International Trade Administration, *US Foreign Trade Highlights, 1992.*

countries because these countries directly supply almost none of the materials and components used in these assembly operations. They are supplied overwhelmingly from Hong Kong (Sung 1991b, 101–02). A significant proportion of the components probably originate in advanced industrial countries, but since they are sold first to Hong Kong firms, these component sales are not reflected in trade data as sales to China. Although adding the value of US goods reexported from Hong Kong to China to the official US data on exports to China, as was done in table 4.2a–c, corrects for the latter problem, it does not adjust for the high import content of a growing share of Chinese exports.

What these two factors mean is that even if China and the United States each had a global trade balance, it is quite likely that the United States would record a large bilateral deficit in its trade with China. Indirect sales via Hong Kong of US products to China, whether finished goods or parts and components, will not be counted in US exports. And indirect imports from China will be counted in US imports.

The larger implication is that bilateral trade data are of diminishing value when capital is highly mobile and where foreign-invested firms, processing and assembly operations, and other types of foreign participation are so important in generating exports. The growing importance of triangular trade through Hong Kong only compounds this problem.

Intellectual Property Rights Protection

China's original commitment to provide copyright, patent, and trademark protection for foreign goods was embodied in the United States–China Bilateral Trade Agreement of 1979. However, efforts to get China to comply with the agreement did not really get under way until the mid-1980s, when the United States raised the issue in meetings of the bilateral Joint Commission on Commerce and Trade. Although some progress was made—China enacted new trademark and patent laws and joined the Paris Convention for the Protection of Intellectual Property—serious shortcomings remained.

In May 1991 the United States government initiated a Special 301 investigation of protection of US intellectual property rights (IPR) in China. Under the Special 301 provision of the Omnibus Trade and Competitiveness Act of 1988, the United States reserves the right to unilaterally impose prohibitive tariffs on designated imports from other countries if an investigation establishes that violations of US intellectual property have occurred.

Six rounds of bilateral negotiations were conducted, leading to the signing of a memorandum of understanding in January 1992. China agreed to make significant improvements in its patent, copyright, and trade secret laws. The major outstanding issue in the patent area had been China's inadequate protection of pharmaceutical and chemical products. The Patent Law of 1984 provided patent rights only to processes to make pharmaceutical and chemical products rather than to the products themselves. Since these products frequently can be produced by more than one method, most US firms found these process patents to be of little value. The memorandum of understanding on intellectual property committed China to provide product patent protection beginning on 1 January 1993.

In the area of copyrights, China agreed to adhere to international standards by joining the Berne Copyright Convention and the Geneva Phonograms Convention. This required amendments of China's copyright law so that computer software would be treated as a literary work and thus subject to copyright protection with a term of 50 years.

US companies and several trade associations hailed the bilateral IPR agreement as an important breakthrough. The International Intellectual Property Alliance, which represents eight US trade associations dealing with the publishing, software, information technology, motion picture, film marketing, business equipment, and recording industries applauded the substance of the agreement, as did the Pharmaceutical Manufacturers Association.

China has carried out all the institutional and legal changes required by the bilateral agreement. China joined the Berne Convention and the Universal Copyright Convention in October 1992 (*National Trade Estimate Report on Foreign Trade Barriers*, Office of the US Trade Representative 1993, 55). In September 1992 the Standing Committee of the National People's Congress amended China's 1984 Patent Law to provide the protection agreed to for chemical and pharmaceutical products and extended the term of protection from the previous 15 years to 20. The new provisions went into effect at the beginning of 1993, as agreed to in the memorandum. China in February 1993 also amended its Trademark

Law, which was first implemented in 1983, to strengthen substantially protection for registered trademarks. Finally, in late 1993 China implemented a new unfair-competition law that improves protection for trade secrets.

Although the appropriate legal structure has been established, enforcement of the provisions of the new laws remains partial. China in mid-1993 did set up its first specialized intellectual property rights court in Beijing to deal with the growing case load. That court heard about 100 cases in 1993 and expected to hear 250 in 1994. However, China continues to be a major producer of pirated compact discs and computer software, a large portion apparently produced in joint venture firms with Taiwanese and Hong Kong partners. US businesses and the Business Software Alliance, a trade group, have called on the US Trade Representative (USTR) to impose sanctions against Chinese goods under the Special 301 provision of the trade law. Thus, discussions on enforcement of the bilateral agreement on intellectual property rights continue. The main US objectives are increased enforcement of existing laws by the Chinese government and the imposition of criminal rather than civil penalties on copyright violators.

Market Access

Bilateral discussions to improve market access in China also began in the mid-1980s in several high-level bilateral forums. However, as noted, the imbalance in bilateral trade continued to widen, leading the United States to initiate more formal bilateral discussions on market access issues in mid-1991. The US objective was to get the Chinese authorities to reduce the number and severity of administrative barriers they imposed on imports. These included import licensing requirements; selective quantitative restrictions on imports; onerous technical barriers, such as product testing and certification requirements; and a lack of transparency (i.e., many internal regulations are not readily available to foreigners) in China's trade regime.

The initial rounds of talks in June and August 1991 in Beijing and in Washington, respectively, were not productive. As a result, the US government in October 1991 initiated an investigation of China's market barriers to US exports under Section 301 of the Trade Act of 1974.

After 10 months of unproductive negotiations, USTR announced on 21 August 1992 a list of $3.9 billion in Chinese exports to the United States that could face prohibitive tariffs if the Chinese failed to reach an agreement with the United States in market access talks.

On 10 October 1992, an agreement, reflected in a memorandum of understanding, was reached between the two governments. The terms of the agreement were quite far-reaching. The United States agreed to terminate the Section 301 investigation and not to impose the prohibitive tariffs on Chinese goods announced in August. The Chinese agreed to dismantle, over five years, 90 percent of all import restrictions, including licensing requirements, quotas, controls, and so forth. In addition, they agreed to eliminate import substitution regulations, to reduce tariffs, and to eliminate the import regulatory tax. The Chinese also agreed to increase the transparency of their trading system by publishing all laws, regulations, policies, and guidance on the operation of their import and export system. This includes a commitment to provide information of commercial interest to US companies, such as the types of products that the state has authorized for purchase from abroad each year and government projects in which imported products may be necessary. The Chinese agreed that all sanitary and phytosanitary standards and testing would be based on sound science and administered so as to avoid creating barriers to the import of US agricultural products such as citrus fruits, stone fruit, apples, grapes, wheat, and tobacco.

The Chinese received from the United States several assurances in return. The most important undoubtedly was that "the U.S. Government will staunchly support China's achievement of contracting party status to the GATT and will work constructively with the Chinese Government and other GATT contracting parties to reach agreement on an acceptable 'Protocol' and then China's rapid attainment of contracting party status" (Memorandum of Understanding Between the Government of the United States of America and the Government of the People's Republic of China Concerning Market Access, USTR, 10 October 1992, 5).

The United States also agreed in the 1992 market access agreement to liberalize the export restrictions that limit Chinese access to technology. Three separate steps were envisioned. First, China would benefit from any liberalization of export control lists and procedures administered through the Coordinating Committee for Multilateral Export Controls (COCOM). Second, in concert with COCOM, China would be eligible for liberalized treatment of computer exports for civilian end users. Finally, the United States agreed to significantly liberalize controls on the export of telecommunications equipment and technology. As will be discussed in chapter 5, by early 1994 the United States had taken several steps to fulfill this obligation.

Although it has required protracted and difficult bilateral negotiations, China by and large has lived up to the terms of the market access agreement. The agreed-upon reductions in the number of imports subject to quotas and licenses have been implemented, and quota levels are being increased for those products for which the elimination of quotas is scheduled for later years. The Chinese have also improved the transparency of their system by more prompt publication of trade regulations.

They have fallen short of US expectations in at least two respects. Most important, they have made very little if any progress in increasing the transparency of the process through which Chinese end users receive approval for imports that remain subject to restrictions such as licensing and quotas. Second, China still restricts certain imports, such as California fruit, on the basis of phytosanitary standards that the United States does not believe meet the standard of being based on "sound scientific evidence." Since the agreement's provisions stretch over several more years, continued bilateral negotiations will be needed to resolve these problems and to monitor compliance more generally.

Trade in Textiles

Textiles have been a source of friction in bilateral US-China trade since the late 1970s. In late 1977, the first petition was filed with the US International Trade Commission against a textile import from China, under Section 406 of the Trade Act of 1974, which deals with market disruption by imports from communist countries (Tsao 1987, 115). Although the ITC found in its investigation that there was no market disruption, frictions in textile trade continued. Early attempts to negotiate a bilateral agreement restricting the flow of Chinese textiles to the United States failed, and in 1979 the United States unilaterally imposed quantitative restrictions on nine textile product categories.

In September 1980 the first formal bilateral textile agreement was reached. It allowed the quota restrictions imposed on six product categories to increase at an annual rate of from 3 to 4 percent over the life of the agreement. However, Chinese exports of items not subject to restrictions under the agreement skyrocketed. In 1981, the first full year of the new agreement, Chinese sales of textiles in the US market increased by two-thirds. In response to pressure from the American textile industry, the US government sought to negotiate a more restrictive agreement to go into effect in 1983, after the expiration of the initial agreement. In talks that opened in August 1982, the United States sought both to increase the number of product categories covered by the agreement and to restrict the allowed growth rate for exports of these products to 1 percent annually over the course of the agreement. The Chinese refused, and in January 1983 a new unilateral agreement was imposed on China with a substantial increase in the number of product categories subject to quantitative restrictions. The Chinese retaliated by suspending their imports from the United States of chemical fibers, cotton, soybeans, and wheat. This was a skillful tactic since at the time China was one of the largest international markets for these products.

Under substantial pressure from influential senior senators and congressmen from farm states, the executive branch negotiated a new bilateral textile agreement that was far more favorable to China. Shortly after the agreement was reached in August 1983, the Chinese resumed purchases of the US goods they had been boycotting. However, the trend of increasing US import restrictions continued. By 1986, 90 percent of all Chinese textile products sold in the United States market were subject to controls. In 1987 the United States imposed quotas for the first time on six categories of textile products fabricated from ramie and ramie-blend fibers. These had not previously been restricted, but in 1986 the revised Multi-Fiber Agreement adopted by the GATT was extended to cover ramie and flax.

One of the most troubling aspects of the textile trade has been China's unwillingness or inability to carry out fully the terms of the bilateral textile agreements reached within the framework of the MFA. The US Customs Service, in order to enforce the quantitative restrictions that the United States imposes on the more than three dozen countries with which it has bilateral agreements covering textile imports, relies on certificates that identify the country of origin of all textile and apparel products coming into the United States. These certificates of origin are provided by the government of each textile-producing country to that country's exporters.

The United States has toughened the country of origin rules over time. For example, in 1984 the United States determined that some textile and apparel products that previously had been considered of Hong Kong origin would henceforth be considered Chinese and counted against China's quotas in the US market. The new criterion was that unless apparel was "substantially transformed" in Hong Kong, it would count against China's quotas. For example, under the old system, bodies of sweaters and sleeves produced in China were shipped to Hong Kong, sewn together, and exported as Hong Kong sweaters. The new system treats such products as Chinese.

Once stricter country-of-origin rules were imposed, Chinese textile and garment producers increasingly resorted to outright fraudulent practices in order to increase their sales to the US market. The most common method was to transship goods through other countries that were not fully using their US quotas. US Customs investigations in 1991 revealed that this was a pervasive practice. In retaliation, the United States cut China's 1991 quotas for cotton sweaters, pants, work towels, and other items by up to 50 percent.

US investigations of these practices led Customs and the Internal Revenue Service to launch a massive operation called Operation Q-Tip, in which the agencies executed 139 search warrants for businesses involved in importing and marketing of Chinese textiles in the United States in September and December 1991. Several of the businesses were either sales agents or subsidiaries of Chinese state trading or textile corporations. The US government charged that they had undervalued Chinese shipments of textiles and garments by as much as $2.1 billion, thus avoiding at least $240 million in customs duties. In January 1992 a

Chinese textile company, two of its US affiliates, and four individuals were indicted on charges of conspiracy to defraud the US government. But by the end of 1993, more than two years after the enforcement operation was launched, the Customs Service had sustained convictions in only one case involving two companies and two individuals, who were found guilty of illegal imported textiles transactions of only $2.7 million, a minuscule fraction of the claimed total violations ("Trade Quotas Build New Chinese Wall," *Wall Street Journal*, 10 January 1994).[2]

The continuing problem of illegal transshipments of Chinese textiles to the United States via third countries was the main focus of bilateral talks beginning in the fall of 1993. The talks were intended to reach a new textile agreement to replace the previous agreement, which expired at the end of 1993. The US government charged that illegal transshipments amounted to as much as $2 billion annually, on top of $4.5 billion in sales that were in compliance with the quotas specified in the bilateral textile agreement. Although the Chinese government has imposed substantial fines and withdrawn the textile trading rights of a number of textile-producing enterprises it had found guilty of illegal third-country transshipments, the United States regarded these enforcement efforts as minimal. It sought to make the Chinese government fully responsible for controlling the transshipment problem, threatening to substantially reduce Chinese quotas and eliminate the annual growth in all product categories if the Chinese government refused to take responsibility for the evasion of US quotas.

The Chinese government does not deny that illegal transshipments have occurred, but it challenges the US estimate of the magnitude of the problem. The inability of US Customs to obtain more convictions in the wake of its massive 1991 enforcement action lends at least some credence to these claims. Moreover, the Chinese government has countered that illegal transshipments were the result of collusion of individual textile factories, many of which were not state-owned, and traders and middlemen over which the government had no effective control. The evasion of China's textile quotas probably involved trading companies not controlled by the Chinese government, including some in third countries, and may have required the cooperation of large US retailers. The Chinese argued that the burden of enforcing the quota restrictions should be shared and that the United States and China also needed to jointly seek cooperation from third countries.

The United States rejected this view and after negotiations broke down in late 1993 announced in early January 1994 that it would unilaterally impose reductions of from 25 to 35 percent on 88 categories of

---

2. In a second case, a US subsidiary of China's state-owned textile corporation was convicted, but the conviction was overturned on a technicality. The Justice Department has indicated that it will seek to retry that case.

textile and apparel products. A slight delay in the scheduled implementation of the quota reductions suggested that the penalties were designed to encourage the Chinese to return to the bargaining table. Indeed, an agreement averting an anticipated $1 billion reduction in the sale of Chinese textiles and apparel in the US market was reached in mid-January 1994. The agreement substantially tightens access to the US market by freezing quotas for 1994 at the same level as 1993 and then allows growth of only 1 percent annually in 1995 and 1996, down substantially from the 4.4 percent annual increases allowed under the previous agreement. In addition, the new agreement was expanded to cover sales of silk apparel for the first time. The Chinese also agreed to accept a provision that will allow the United States to reduce China's quota by an amount equal to three times the value of any future illegal transshipments.

Currency Manipulation

Under the provisions of the 1988 trade act, the US Department of the Treasury is required to assess annually whether US trading partners manipulate their exchange rates in order to prevent effective balance of payments adjustment or to gain unfair competitive advantage in international trade. Each annual report is issued in November and updated in May. Since the fall 1990 report, which was the first to consider China, the Treasury has been an increasingly harsh critic of China's foreign exchange regime. In May 1992 the department concluded, for the first time, that China was manipulating its exchange rate. This assessment was reiterated the following year, both in Treasury's spring and fall official reports and by Under Secretary for International Affairs Lawrence Summers, who testified before the Subcommittee on International Finance and Monetary Policy of the Senate Committee on Banking, Housing, and Urban Affairs on 25 May 1993 that Chinese manipulation of its exchange rate and its currency reserves impeded US exports to China.

There certainly is no doubt that the Chinese government for years has fixed the official exchange rate and has intervened in the secondary market for foreign exchange in a variety of ways to manipulate what is usually referred to as the swap market rate (Lardy 1992b, 61–63, 120–21, 160–61). However, the government invariably intervened to prevent a further depreciation of the swap market rate. And the gap between the official and swap market rate, which existed until the two rates were unified at the higher swap market rate at the beginning of 1994, showed that the official rate overvalued the Chinese currency, thus taxing Chinese exporters and indirectly subsidizing Chinese imports. Thus the interventions and manipulation would likely have the opposite effect of that postulated by the US Department of the Treasury.

This conclusion is certainly borne out by an analysis of developments in 1992 and 1993. In 1992 the acceleration of economic growth in China significantly eroded China's trade surplus, which had reached a reform-era peak in 1990 (table 2.1). That trend was even more evident in 1993. This led to pressure on the value of the *renminbi* on the secondary market. "By the end of February 1993 the value of the currency on the secondary market had depreciated about 43 percent in nominal terms compared to the end of 1991, and the gap between the average swap market rate and the official rate widened to over 45.8 percent" (World Bank 1993b, 16).

In response to this pressure, the State Administration of Exchange Control took a number of measures to prevent a further slide in the value of the *renminbi*. These included placing a price ceiling of about 8 yuan per dollar on transactions in the secondary market and encouraging state enterprises to sell their foreign exchange holdings. The state also appears to have sold several hundred million dollars in an attempt to prop up the value of the *renminbi*.

The effect of these measures was predictable. Volume on the swap market dried up as those holding foreign exchange refused to sell at what they regarded as too low a price, and black market activity in foreign exchange soared.

In June 1993 the government abandoned its attempt to control the market. The very first day after controls were lifted, the value of the currency slid from 8.1 to 10.2 on the Shanghai market. The value of the domestic currency fell by about one-quarter within a few days on all markets. Predictably, transaction volume also soared. In Shanghai, the single largest foreign exchange market, for example, in the first seven trading days in June the volume of transactions was equal to 60 percent of all transactions in the first five months of the year.

Not surprisingly, the immediate response to the lifting of price controls proved to be an overshooting of the equilibrium exchange rate. By mid-June the swap market rate had stabilized at about Y8.8. The strengthening of the *renminbi* reflected not only a correction of the initial overshooting of the exchange rate but monetary and credit tightening initiated in May. As firms found it increasingly difficult to get domestic currency loans, they sold their foreign exchange holdings for domestic currency. In addition, the strengthening also reflected the effect of a new regulation of the State Administration of Exchange Control that required exporters to use or sell their foreign exchange holdings within a period of several months, which increased the supply of foreign exchange on the market.

However, since the official exchange rate changed little during 1993, there remained a considerable gap between that rate and the swap market price of foreign exchange, reflecting the undervaluation of the official exchange rate.

The Treasury, in its analysis of China's exchange rate, appears not to have fully taken into account the increasing decentralization of China's foreign exchange market and the increasing role of exchange rate expectations in the determination of the swap market rate. They argued that rising official foreign exchange reserves in 1992 placed additional pressure on the value of the *renminbi* in the secondary market. In short, had reserves been unchanged, more foreign exchange would have been available to finance imports, the depreciation of the currency in the swap market would have been less, and China's trade surplus in 1992 would have been smaller. All else being equal, US firms probably would have sold more goods to China, and the US deficit would have been smaller.

The problem with this line of analysis is that it fails to take into account the heterogeneity of what is referred to as China's international reserves. At the outset of reform, reserves were quite small, and gold (valued at the London price) comprised two-thirds of the total. By the end of 1992, total international reserves had increased more than tenfold compared with 1978, and less than 10 percent of the total was official holdings of gold. Foreign exchange reserves of more than $45 billion had come to comprise almost 90 percent of total reserves (World Bank 1993b, 104).

However, less than half of these foreign exchange reserves were foreign exchange holdings of China's central bank, the People's Bank of China. The majority of foreign exchange reserves consisted of the net foreign exchange position of the Bank of China, China's principal foreign exchange bank. The Bank's net foreign exchange position consists of deposits of foreign exchange in the domestic and foreign branches of the bank minus its net loans of foreign exchange. Its domestic deposits of foreign exchange include those of foreign-invested firms that maintained foreign exchange accounts at the Bank of China; individual savers, whose deposits had reached more than $6 billion by the end of 1992 and rose by another $2.6 billion in the first 10 months of 1993; the almost 4,000 Chinese foreign trade corporations; and several hundred manufacturing enterprises authorized to enter directly into foreign trade transactions. In addition, some of the other specialized banks held much smaller amounts of foreign exchange deposits.

Although the state could influence the size of the foreign exchange holdings of some domestic depositors, the extent of control diminished rapidly in the 1980s. At the outset of reform, there were only a dozen foreign trade companies, and they were probably the source of most of the foreign exchange deposits in the Bank of China. Since these companies were controlled directly by the Ministry of Foreign Economic Relations and Trade, their foreign exchange holdings for all practical purposes were fully at the disposal of the central government. By the early 1990s, there were thousands of foreign trade companies over which the central government exercised only the most tenuous control. Similarly, at the beginning of reform, individual foreign exchange deposits were negligible; by 1992 they comprised about a sixth of total foreign exchange reserves.

These developments appear to underlie the 1992 decision of the Chinese authorities to redefine their measure of official international reserves as the sum of state reserves (i.e., foreign exchange holdings of the People's Bank of China), gold, China's reserve position in the International Monetary Fund, and holdings of Special Drawing Rights (SDRs). Thus, since August 1992 China's reporting of its reserves to the IMF excludes the net foreign exchange position of the Bank of China.

Since import decisions are now very decentralized, it is probably appropriate to continue to use a broad definition of reserves in calculating how many months of import cover China has available—that is, the number of months of imports that could be paid for from all available sources of foreign exchange. It is appropriate because much of the net foreign exchange position of the Bank of China represents the foreign exchange holdings of importers such as foreign trade corporations, enterprises with direct trading rights, or firms that have exported and are holding retained foreign exchange to finance imports. These importers finance a large share of their imports from the foreign exchange reserves they control themselves, not from foreign exchange supplied from state reserves under the plan.

It appears to be less appropriate to follow the US Treasury Department's practice of using changes in the level of a broad definition of reserves in assessing the central government's influence over or manipulation of the official exchange rate. That is because the government's direct control is limited to foreign exchange reserves held by the central bank. Since state foreign exchange reserves (i.e., foreign exchange holdings of the central bank) actually fell by $2.27 billion in 1992 and continued to fall in the first half of 1993, it would appear that the actions of the central government tended to mitigate the rate of decline in the value of the domestic currency. In other words, in the absence of official dollar sales, the domestic currency would have depreciated more, exports would have been greater, imports would have been smaller, and the trade surplus larger. In the first half of 1993, the trade deficit would have been smaller.

The main reason that total foreign exchange reserves rose even as the central government trimmed its official foreign exchange holdings was exchange rate expectations. Under pressure from the European Community to move to a unitary exchange rate and make the currency convertible, Chinese officials in 1992 began to openly discuss convertibility as a goal. Similarly, both the United States and the European Community were demanding that China reduce and eventually eliminate almost all import quotas and import licensing requirements as a condition for participating in the GATT.

Exporters and individual holders of foreign exchange anticipated that moving to convertibility and eliminating import controls would be accompanied by depreciation in the value of the currency, so they took two actions. First, they refrained from selling their holdings of foreign exchange. Their foreign exchange holdings appear to have increased by $7.1 billion in 1992. This would have been impossible in the prereform era because producers of export goods and those individuals who received remittances from their relatives overseas had to surrender 100 percent of their foreign exchange to the government. But under the much more decentralized conditions created by reform, exporters have been allowed to retain a growing share of their earnings. Beginning in 1992, the requirement to surrender foreign exchange at the official exchange rate was reduced to 20 percent of export earnings. The central government retained the right to purchase an additional 30 percent, but such transactions were at the higher swap rate. As early as the mid-1980s, individuals receiving remittances from their relatives abroad also were allowed to retain the entire amount in foreign exchange, one of the reasons for the burgeoning individual foreign exchange deposits at the Bank of China.

Second, those that had foreign exchange moved record amounts offshore. Errors and omissions in the balance of payments accounts for 1992 jumped to an astounding -$12.2 billion according to the World Bank, presumably largely reflecting unrecorded capital outflows. In the Bank's view, because of "the increasing complexity of the linkages between the mainland and Hong Kong financial markets, there now exist numerous legal and illegal channels for funds to move in and out of China." These outflows more than offset the record officially reported inflows of foreign direct investment so that "China in fact recorded net capital outflows by end-1992, instead of the net inflows indicated by the official statistics" (World Bank 1993b, 14). Large capital outflows appear to have continued in 1993.

In short, exchange rate expectations in an environment of substantial decentralization of control of foreign exchange earnings appear to be the principal reason for the slide in the value of the *renminbi* in 1992 and 1993. The direct actions of the central government almost certainly held down the rate of depreciation of the currency in 1992 and probably also in 1993. In view of this, it seems difficult to sustain the US Treasury's charge that the actions of the Chinese government curtailed US exports.

Services

A major objective of US policy is that US firms operating abroad should receive what is called national treatment. This means that US firms operating in China should be subject to no more restrictions and regulations than comparable Chinese firms face. Although the Chinese accepted this general principle in the bilateral trade agreement signed in 1979, achieving this objective has proved extraordinarily difficult. Problems exist in many areas, but the most important are banking, insurance, shipping, and civil aviation.

Banking

Although a number of US banks operate representative offices in China, the range of services that they are allowed to provide is extremely limited. Most importantly, they are not allowed to accept domestic currency deposits or to make loans denominated in domestic currency. That means that their primary activity is taking foreign currency deposits and making foreign currency loans to foreign-invested enterprises.

Insurance

Although the license the US firm AIG received to sell insurance in 1992 was something of a breakthrough, this sector is still almost completely monopolized by the People's Insurance Company. AIG is allowed to sell only two lines of insurance and in a single city, Shanghai, so that most of the market remains the exclusive purview of the Chinese.

Shipping

A new bilateral maritime agreement was signed in December 1988, replacing an earlier agreement that had expired in 1983. The 1988 agreement provided greater access to the Chinese market for US shipping companies. This paved the way for shipping companies to open representative offices and start feeder services out of Chinese ports. However, a number of other restrictive practices remained and were not resolved in bilateral discussions in the fall of 1990. Thus the US Federal Maritime Commission launched a formal investigation of China's shipping practices in July 1991. In February 1992 the investigation was concluded in light of the Chinese agreeing in October 1991, for the first time, to allow wholly foreign-owned shipping enterprises to operate in China, thus allowing foreign firms to solicit cargoes directly. The agreement was extended for another year on 28 September 1992.

Yet to be fully resolved is the right of US carriers to offer inland trucking—that is, freight forwarding services—to complement their shipping activities. Based on the terms of the September 1992 extension, US companies such as Sealand expected to be able to offer such services between Hong Kong and Canton, the capital of Guangdong Province, starting 1 March 1993 but were blocked by the provincial government, presumably to protect the interests of Sinotrans, a government shipping agency. To overcome this barrier, Sealand eventually entered into a joint venture agreement with Sinotrans to carry freight between Canton and Hong Kong. Thus it appears that local government authorities prevented the full implementation of the bilateral maritime agreement.

Civil Aviation

A final area of bilateral dispute in services has been civil aviation. The first bilateral agreement on civil air transport, signed 17 January 1980, led to the opening of air service between the two countries. Negotiations in October 1990 led to amendments, adopted in February 1992, that increased the frequency of air service, expanded the number of routes, and added an unrestricted all-cargo route.

In 1993 a new American carrier sought to open the all-cargo route to China but was unable to do so. In retaliation, the US Department of Transportation announced it would suspend the landing rights of all-cargo flights operated by China Eastern, a Shanghai-based company. The day before the suspension was to take effect, the United States lifted its suspension threat, in response to progress in the discussions between the Chinese authorities and the American company to open the new service. The all-cargo service of the Oregon-based Evergreen Company started shortly thereafter and has been operating without difficulty since.

Export Controls and Proliferation Sanctions

The United States imposed an embargo on all trade with China from the time of the Korean War until mid-1971. Since the embargo was lifted, exports to China, like those to other communist states, have been subject to a complex system that restricts exports of goods, services, and technology with military or dual-use military and civilian application. Controls on military items are enforced by the US Department of State, in accordance with the provisions of the Arms Export Control Act. With the concurrence of the Department of Defense, State maintains the US Munitions List (USML) (General Accounting Office 1993a, 2). Controls on dual-use items are enforced through licensing requirements administered by US government agencies within the Departments of Commerce, Defense, Energy, and State (Richardson 1993, 34). These agencies are charged with the administration of the Export Control Act of 1949 and subsequently the Export Administration Act of 1969, the Export Administration Act of 1979, and related legislation. The Department of Commerce takes the lead among these agencies and establishes the Commerce Control List (CCL), which regulates the export of dual-use technologies.

Since 1949 COCOM has been the principal mechanism among the Western allies for coordinating controls on exports of dual-use items to what was at one time called the Sino-Soviet bloc. Although enforcement of the restrictions is the responsibility of each participating country, COCOM serves as a forum for negotiation and consultation among the participants (Kemme 1991, 6).

COCOM maintains three lists of controlled items: the Munitions List, the Atomic Energy List, and the International Industrial List (IIL). The latter regulates the export of high-technology industrial items such as computers, software, telecommunications equipment, machine tools, industrial furnaces, laboratory testing devices, and other items that have potential military applications. The CCL of the Department of Commerce is closely related to the IIL of COCOM.

In addition to COCOM, three other multilateral arrangements exist to control the transfer of dual-use items: the Nuclear Suppliers Group (NSG) for nuclear items, the Australia Group (AG) for chemical and biological items, and the Missile Technology Control Regime (MTCR) for missile systems (Bertsch and Cupitt 1993, 53–54)

US exporters have long argued that, while US export controls on dual-use items, in principle, are multilateral, they nonetheless disadvantage US exporters compared with their competitors. Dissatisfaction stems from a belief that the United States has stricter enforcement than other countries; a slower, less helpful process of providing information on changes in the COCOM export control regime; and a slower, more cumbersome bureaucratic approval process of license approval (Richardson 1993, 35; General Accounting Office 1990).

The view that US enforcement of COCOM provisions is stricter than that of other participants in the COCOM regime stems from at least two factors. First, over the years the CCL and the USML lists in the United States began to overlap. Because restrictions on the USML are more severe than those on the CCL, US controls became more restrictive than COCOM controls as the degree of overlap in the lists increased.

The USML is more restrictive for several reasons. First, the USML restrictions are imposed on exports to all countries, whereas the CCL has been directed primarily toward communist countries. Second, the Department of State has the authority to turn down, revoke, or suspend a license for any product on the USML for any national security or foreign policy reason. By contrast, once issued, licenses for dual-use items controlled by the CCL can not be revoked or suspended unless the president specifically certifies to the Congress that there is a breach of the peace that threatens the strategic interests of the United States. Thus, US industry generally prefers to have items controlled by the Department of Commerce through the CCL rather than by the Department of State through the USML (General Accounting Office 1993a, 4 and 14–15).

A second reason US controls are believed to be stricter stems from the nature of the COCOM's IIL, which has three levels of restriction. The most restrictive items, called general exceptions, basically are embargoed and may be exported to proscribed countries only if the license is reviewed collectively by all participating countries and approved unanimously. The least restrictive category, items controlled by administrative exception notes, covers items that warrant control but that are controlled by each member nation separately, without collective review (General Accounting Office 1993a, 13). US exporters generally believe that the United States controls these latter items more strictly than do other COCOM members.

There is some evidence that US firms are also disadvantaged relative to their competitors in other industrial nations because "the US lags behind other major COCOM countries in both implementing changes and disseminating information to its business community on impending changes resulting from the COCOM list review process" (General Accounting Office 1990, 2). In many other COCOM countries, firms are given advance notice of impending changes to the CCL, and formal notification and implementation of the changes is a simple process that occurs soon after COCOM agreement is reached. By contrast, the US government treats all information and documents generated during the COCOM review process as restricted and refrains from taking any advance steps to inform US firms that changes are pending. Only when the interagency review of COCOM changes is complete and the revised regulations are formally published in the *Federal Register* do US firms learn of the changes. After the 1989 review process, 62 commodity classifications were liberalized. But the US interagency review process for 28 of these commodities was so lengthy that the revised regulations were not published until two months after the effective COCOM date, and for three commodities the delay was seven months (General Accounting Office 1990, 3). In short, US firms are doubly handicapped—they receive no advance notice of impending changes, and not infrequently changes are publicized long after they have taken effect. While US firms are in the dark, foreign firms are negotiating sales with potential foreign customers and consummating agreements that call for shipment of goods on the effective date of the change (General Accounting Office 1990, 4).

The belief that export controls disadvantage US exporters relative to those from other Western countries obviously also stems from well-publicized cases in which controls were imposed unilaterally by the United States at high cost to US firms. In 1978, for example, the Carter administration, in response to the conviction of a Soviet dissident, imposed controls on the sale to the Soviet Union of gas and oil exploration and production equipment. The business immediately went to a French company (Kemme 1991, 8). The United States took unilateral action again after martial law was declared in Poland in December 1981 and banned the sale of US equipment for a Soviet gas pipeline. The United States in June 1982 even sought to extend the ban to encompass goods produced by US subsidiaries abroad and goods produced by foreign firms using licensed US technology. Efforts to impose such unilateral controls were finally abandoned in late 1982 (Kemme 1991, 9). More recently, in 1992 Vietnam Airlines, anticipating the lifting of the US trade embargo, sought to purchase six Boeing 737 aircraft. When President Bush left office without lifting the embargo and it became clear that President Clinton was not going to take early action, the Vietnamese signed a multiyear lease for five A-320s from Airbus in the fall of 1993.

Over time, a number of efforts have been made to reduce the relative disadvantage faced by US exporters. Among the most important was the adoption, in the Export Administration Act of 1969, of the "foreign availability" criterion. This meant, in principle, that if a US exporter could demonstrate to the Department of Commerce that a controlled product was available from an alternative foreign supplier not bound by COCOM regulations, a license could not be denied for national security reasons. When COCOM was formed, its members (initially the NATO countries except for Iceland) had a virtual monopoly on advanced industrial technology. Even though such important sources of dual-use technologies as Japan and Australia later became participants in COCOM, over time other countries—including Brazil, India, Israel, South Korea, and Taiwan—became increasingly significant sources of industrial technology with dual-use applications. These countries were not subject to any COCOM export constraints.

A second major step to reduce the relative disadvantage faced by US exporters occurred in 1991, following COCOM's June 1990 decision to develop a new core list of controlled goods and technologies. The new list relaxed controls on 350 of the 600 dual-use sub-items on the International Industrial List (Bertsch and Cupitt 1993, 54). The US Department of Commerce on 1 June 1991 adopted a new, much shorter, list of controlled exports based on the new COCOM criteria. Most importantly, the revisions succeeded in reducing significantly the number of technologies that were subject to both USML and CCL controls (General Accounting Office 1993a).

Despite the reduction in the number of controlled items, 30 to 40 percent of all US manufactured exports still require validated licenses, down somewhat from the roughly half that required such licenses in the mid-1980s (Richardson 1993, 129). Moreover, the costs of complying with US export controls increasingly have been shifted from US government agencies to US exporters. Richardson (1993, 130), for example, estimates that the cost to high-technology exporters of complying with export controls, especially monitoring export products, customers, and end uses for security and proliferation goals, add 1 percent to variable costs.

With the end of the Cold War, COCOM has undergone significant changes and is scheduled to be replaced in 1994 with a broader group that will still seek to control the flow of certain technologies to specific nations. It seems likely that the replacement for COCOM will permit more favorable treatment of Central European countries in return for their instituting safeguards designed to prevent the diversion of the advanced technology they will be allowed to import. These safeguards will be designed to prevent the diversion of advanced technology to countries such as North Korea, Libya, Iran, Iraq, and Cuba.

Recent experience with China illustrates another important trend. US export controls are turning increasingly toward countering proliferation of weapons of mass destruction and the dual-use products that support such weaponry (Richardson 1993, 129). The terms of the National Defense Authorization Act for fiscal 1991, for example, require the president of the United States to impose sanctions for two years against foreign countries that he determines to be involved in the transfer of missile-related equipment and technology to countries that are not signatories to the Missile Technology Control Regime (MTCR), a 1987 international agreement designed to limit the ability of additional countries to develop missiles with nuclear and chemical warhead capability. The agreement initially restricted the transfer of missiles and missile-related technology capable of delivering a minimum 500-kilogram payload a distance of 300 or more kilometers. In 1993 the agreement was tightened to proscribe the sale of any missile with a range over 300 kilometers or any missile intended for use with a weapon of mass destruction. The particular prohibited items that contribute to missile design, development, or production, which trigger the sanctions, are listed in the MTCR Annex.

President Bush first imposed sanctions tied to proliferation concerns in late April 1991, when he refused to approve an export license for the sale of US components for a Chinese domestic communications satellite. Then in June 1991, under the terms of the Defense Authorization Act, he imposed sanctions against the China Great Wall Industry Corporation, which offers satellite launch services, and the China Precision Machinery Import-Export Corporation, when it was determined that these companies had been involved in the secret delivery of launchers for M-11 missiles to Pakistan. When Secretary of State James Baker visited China in November 1991, he extracted a promise from Chinese leaders that they would adhere to the provisions of the MTCR. But they made this commitment conditional on the United States lifting the specific sanctions that had been imposed in June 1991. In mid-December 1991 the State Department notified Congress of its intention to lift the sanctions, and on 23 March 1992 that was accomplished.

The issue of Chinese violations of the MTCR resurfaced again in late 1992, when it appeared that the Chinese had shipped M-11 missiles, or components for such missiles, to Pakistan. The evidence, however, apparently was ambiguous, and it was not until 25 August 1993 that Under Secretary of State for International Security Affairs Lynn E. Davis announced a formal US government determination that China had violated its agreement to adhere to the terms of the MTCR and imposed new sanctions on technology exports to China.

The August 1993 sanctions ban the sale of almost $1 billion in high-technology goods to China over two years. The sanctions cover rocket systems and subsystems, flight control systems, including reentry vehicles and systems related to warheads. Among the most hard-hit companies will be Hughes Aircraft Company, a major supplier to China of communications satellites and ground stations. Under the terms of the sanctions, Hughes will be allowed to sell items for which licenses had been issued before the sanctions were announced, apparently including a satellite and ground station. However, pending sales of 10 or more satellites, for which licenses had not yet been issued, could be affected if the sanctions remain in place for the full two years, making it more likely that Hughes would lose sales to British and French manufacturers.

Moreover, the reliability of other American suppliers was called into question by the sanctions because other items on the potential sanction list in response to MTCR violations include flight control systems, avionics equipment, launch support equipment, software, and certain computers. Collins Avionics, a unit of Rockwell International, feared that China would reduce its purchases of aircraft equipped with Collins equipment. The fear was palpable because China is Rockwell's most important international market for avionics products.

The Legacy of the 1989 Sanctions

Contrary to common impression, many of the sanctions the US government imposed on China in June 1989 remain in effect. The suspension of the programs in China of the Overseas Private Investment Corporation (OPIC), a US government agency that guarantees private investment against foreign expropriation, was incorporated into the Foreign Relations Act for fiscal 1990–91. The same legislation precludes the US Trade and Development Program, discussed further in chapter 5, from offering financing for industrial feasibility studies.

Similarly, under the provisions of the law, the US government until March 1994 refused to license the sale to China of steam turbines and generators when they would be used in nuclear power generation plants. This is because the Foreign Relations Authorization Act for fiscal 1990–91 suspends all nuclear cooperation between China and the United States. The law does not directly affect the sale of steam turbines, generators, turbine generator sets, and process control systems when such equipment is used in coal-fired plants. But it did restrict the sale of such equipment when used in nuclear power plants even though such steam turbine generators and other equipment are not nuclear technology. Indirectly, the ban may have impeded the sale of such equipment intended for fossil fuel plants as well since "non-U.S. suppliers which can serve both market segments may be able to achieve economies of scale and therefore offer more favorable commercial terms than those available to U.S. companies which are unable by law to serve this market segment" (testimony of John B. Yasinsky before the US Senate Committee on Energy and Natural Resources, 11 March 1993, 35). Thus the the imposition of these sanctions for almost five years may have diminished sales by US firms, such as Westinghouse and the General Electric Company, in what is anticipated will be a $200 billion market over the next 10 years, of which at least 25 percent will consist of new generation capacity ordered from foreign suppliers (testimony of John B. Yasinsky before the US Senate Committee on Energy and Natural Resources, 11 March 1993, 31).

Other sanctions the US government imposed in 1989, however, have been eased on a case-by-case basis, as reflected in special waivers given by the executive branch. The US Export-Import Bank, for example, in 1990 resumed limited lending for exports to China under such a waiver. Cray Research Inc.'s application to sell a supercomputer to China was tied up in the sanctions regime until late 1993, when President Clinton finally announced that the license would be issued, paving the way for the long-pending sale.

Prison Labor Exports

The Tariff Act of 1930, more commonly known as the Smoot-Hawley tariffs, makes the import into the United States of goods produced or mined by convict labor illegal under most circumstances. Although this act has been seized upon by critics of China's human rights practices, it is interesting to note that the prohibition does not cover goods that are judged to be in short supply in the United States—clear evidence that the original intention was not to advance human rights outside the United States but to protect American workers from competition from foreign goods produced in circumstances in which wages could be artificially depressed.

Evidence that some Chinese goods imported into the United States were produced in prison-run factories first surfaced in the late 1980s. Bilateral discussions led to the signing of a memorandum of understanding between the United States and China on this issue on 7 August 1992. The Chinese pledged to take steps to halt such exports and agreed that the United States could post a US Customs official in the American Embassy in Beijing. That official was to have access to facilities suspected of using prison labor to produce products for export.

The Chinese have reiterated a domestic law forbidding the export of goods produced in prisons, have ruled that prisons are not allowed to enter into joint ventures with foreign firms, and have gradually come into compliance with the memorandum. US Customs officials complained that after their initial inspection in the spring of 1993 of two prisons suspected of producing export products they were not allowed to visit additional sites—a complaint that high administration officials reiterated. In retrospect, it is clear that the Chinese refused to approve the visits to additional prisons because the results of the initial inspections had not been released. After a delay of almost eight and a half months, the commissioner of US Customs finally released the report on the first inspection, admitting that it had found no evidence the inspected factories were using prison labor (*Federal Register* 58, no. 237, 13 December 1993, 65235). Shortly thereafter, the Chinese agreed to the inspection of additional factories suspected of producing goods with convict labor.

Most-Favored Nation Status

Under the terms of the Jackson-Vanik Amendment to the Trade Act of 1974, MFN can be extended to nonmarket economies only if the president issues a waiver certifying either that the country does not impede emigration or that providing MFN status likely will lead to increased emigration. Once MFN status is awarded to a nonmarket economy, it must be renewed annually. In the Chinese case, since MFN status expires on 3 July every year, the law requires the president to state his intention to renew the waiver by 3 June. If the Congress objects to continued MFN status for China it must pass a joint resolution disapproving the waiver by 1 September. The president has the option of vetoing the joint resolution, in which case Congress has 15 legislative days to override the veto, which requires a two-thirds vote in both the House and Senate. If an override vote were successful, China's MFN status would expire 60 days after the vote.

China first gained MFN status in the US market in 1980. The process of renewal was routine. While there was no doubt China was a nonmarket economy, the emigration issue was defused by Deng Xiaoping's offer to allow as many as 10 million Chinese to emigrate to the United States. Renewal has become highly controversial since Tiananmen because many congressmen and, more recently, the executive branch have come to view the threat of withdrawing China's MFN status in the US market as a major lever to encourage the Chinese government to improve human rights, to limit the spread of nuclear weapons, and to further open China's market to US goods in order to reduce the large and growing bilateral trade imbalance.

Ironically, the original intention of the Jackson-Vanik Amendment has been forgotten. On the basis of the original emigration criterion, there is no doubt that China qualifies for MFN status because Chinese emigration to the United States is restricted primarily by US immigration policy rather than by Chinese emigration policy. Under the US Immigration Act of 1990, a maximum number of 270,000 immigrant visas can be issued annually under what is referred to as the worldwide limitation. Within this overall limitation, no more than 20,000 visas can be issued to natives of any single country (*Statistical Yearbook of the Immigration and Naturalization Service*, 1992, 17). However, immediate relatives of US citizens, refugees, and a select number of others are exempt from the worldwide limitation.

In fiscal 1991, 33,025 Chinese immigrated to the United States, making China the ninth largest source of immigrants. Of these, 19,118 entered subject to the numerical limitation of 20,000 annually, and 13,907 were exempt, almost all because they were immediate relatives of US citizens (*Statistical Yearbook of the Immigration and Naturalization Service*, 1992, 20). Since visas are valid for four months after they are issued and, if issued toward the end of any fiscal year, may be used in either of two years, the admission in 1991 of more than 19,000 immigrants not subject to the numerical limitation suggests that the 20,000 annual visa limit is the biggest constraint to Chinese immigration. In short, the annual number of Chinese citizens who have the approval of their government to emigrate to the United States far exceeds the number the US government is prepared to admit.

For Chinese who are not immediate relatives of US citizens, the main loophole for would-be immigrants seeking to get around the US numerical limitation has been to enter the United States illegally and apply for political asylum, either voluntarily or after apprehension by US authorities. Until the Clinton administration tightened the criteria for awarding political asylum in 1993, this was a fairly easy route. In the 12 months ending 30 September 1992, 85 percent of all those voluntary Chinese applicants to the US Immigration and Naturalization Service were awarded political asylum. The most common grounds was the assertion that they faced persecution if they returned to China because they had violated state family planning policies—the one-child norm, in particular. A third of those apprehended while trying to enter the United States also were awarded political asylum ("U.S. Cutting Back on Generosity in Granting of Asylum for Chinese Refugees," *New York Times*, 5 September 1993).

But beginning in 1993, a new, tougher policy seemed to be taking shape. Most of the 256 survivors from the Golden Venture, a ship laden with Chinese that ran aground off the Rockaway Peninsula in Queens in June 1993, were kept in detention, and the Immigration and Naturalization Service sought to return them to China on the grounds that they had not adequately demonstrated that they had been singled out by the Chinese government for persecution for a political or religious belief.

A federal judge in early 1994 rejected this view, arguing that opposition to the Chinese government's policies of population control does constitute an expression of political opinion ("Judge Allows Asylum over Birth Policy," *New York Times*, 21 January 1994). The Department of Justice may appeal the decision, and it is not binding on other cases, so the effect of the ruling on the likelihood of illegal immigrants from China being awarded political asylum will not be clear for some time.

Even as the US government maintained a restrictive quota on immigration and sought to impose tougher standards on Chinese seeking political asylum, US Secretary of State Warren Christopher informed the Chinese government on several occasions in the latter part of 1993 and in early 1994 that MFN would not be renewed in June 1994 unless it improves human rights conditions, conforms to the standards of the Missile Technology Control Regime, and further reforms its trading practices. None of these was envisaged in the Jackson-Vanik Amendment as a criterion for extending MFN trading status to nonmarket economies. However, as will be discussed in chapter 5, all were included in President Clinton's May 1993 executive order extending China's MFN status through the middle of 1994.

Economic Consequences of Discontinuing China's MFN Status

Estimates of the decline in Chinese exports to the United States as a consequence of loss of MFN status in the US market vary, depending on the assumptions underlying the analysis and several other variables. Moreover, a discontinuation of China's MFN status almost certainly would lead to retaliatory action by the Chinese, which would substantially reduce US exports to China. Since the scope of the Chinese retaliatory action would be a Chinese decision, the size of the ultimate reduction in bilateral trade caused by the termination of China's MFN status in the US market would be determined as much by political as economic factors.

Even estimating the latter is complex because there would be important follow-on effects to any initial reduction in bilateral trade flows. For example, reduced Chinese exports to the United States would have a substantial effect on economic growth in Hong Kong.

In 1993 the Hong Kong government estimated that a loss of China's MFN status in the United States would reduce reexports from China to the United States by 34 to 47 percent or by $6.1 billion to $8.6 billion per year. That would mean a loss of income and employment in Hong Kong and thus a reduction in the rate of economic growth in Hong Kong by 2.2 to 3.1 percentage points. That represents between two-fifths and three-fifths of Hong Kong's underlying rate of growth in recent years. US exports to Hong Kong in 1992, exclusive of those reexported to China, were valued at $6.7 billion. The curtailment in Hong Kong's growth at the margin would reduce the demand for US goods in Hong Kong, resulting in further job losses in the United States beyond those attributable to the direct reduction in Chinese purchases of US goods.

The immediate effect of a loss of MFN status for Chinese goods in the United States would be higher prices for US consumers and thus reduced sales by the Chinese into the US market. The amount by which prices would rise can be estimated based on the increased tariff rates associated with non-MFN status. Non-MFN tariff rates are five to ten times as high as prevailing MFN tariff rates. For example, for toys, a major Chinese export, the MFN tariff is 7.4 percent; the non-MFN rate is 55 percent. For apparel, the tariff rates are 15.3 percent and 55 percent, respectively. The actual price increase at the retail level, of course, would depend on the share of the total price represented by the goods as opposed to distribution costs, markups, and so forth.

In addition, the price increase would depend on the elasticity of Chinese export supply. If Chinese prices fell as a result of reduced demand from the US market, then the ultimate upward influence on prices of Chinese goods in the United States would be moderated.

Finally, one needs to take into account the elasticity of substitution between Chinese exports and those of competing suppliers. If the shifting of demand from Chinese to other suppliers has a large upward effect on the prices of those suppliers, then Chinese goods would be relatively less disadvantaged in the US market. On the other hand, if the elasticity of supply from other countries is quite high, the price of the product in the US market would rise less, but purchases from China would fall more—that is, the elasticity of substitution would be higher.

In addition to these three factors, the amount by which sales of Chinese goods would be reduced in the US market also depends on the price elasticity of demand. Most of China's exports to the United States—low-end quality textiles and apparel, relatively inexpensive footwear and leather goods, relatively simple toys, and so forth—are relatively price-sensitive, so higher prices would reduce sales significantly.

Estimates of the amount by which Chinese exports would initially be reduced range from about $6 billion to as much as $15 billion. Perhaps the most comprehensive and methodologically most sophisticated estimate was made by the World Bank. Based on actual US imports in 1990 of 15 key products totaling $8.6 billion, estimated US price elasticities of demand, estimated elasticities of Chinese export supply, and estimated elasticities of substitution between Chinese exports and those of competing suppliers, the Bank concluded that Chinese sales in the US market would have been 43 to 96 percent less in 1990 if non-MFN tariffs had been in effect. On the assumption that other Chinese exports to the

United States would experience the same proportional decline, the Bank estimated that the total reduction in Chinese exports would have been between $7 billion and $15.2 billion. The report concludes that dislocations of trade flows as a result of the discontinuation of China's MFN status "would range from the dramatic to the disastrous" (World Bank 1993a, 155–58).

Each estimate of the likely degree of trade disruption in the event of the discontinuation of China's MFN trading status in the US market is a function of its particular assumptions. However, on balance, there can be little doubt that the reduction of Chinese sales in the US market would be massive. Prices of Chinese goods would rise considerably and, given the price sensitivity of demand for most of these commodities, sales inevitably would fall sharply. Likely Chinese retaliation, in the form of reduced purchases of US products, would further curtail bilateral trade and, if severe, would likely lead to a downward spiral in the entire bilateral economic relationship. Recommendations that are designed to avoid this scenario are advanced in chapter 5.

5

Conclusions and Policy Implications

China is likely to be an increasingly important trading country. Based on the analysis in chapter 2, China's exports are likely to continue to grow by 10 to 15 percent annually, and thus trade value in 1995 is likely to be between $220 billion and $250 billion. If the latter projection is true, China's exports in 1995 would be about the level of Japan's in 1980. If the higher rate of expansion were continued to the end of the decade, China's trade would double again, putting it at roughly the level of Japan in 1989.

In short, barring disruptions that would ensue from the loss of most-favored nation (MFN) status in the US market or a more protectionist international trading system and assuming appropriate macroeconomic and exchange rate policies in China, China's importance as a trading nation in 1995 will lag that of Japan by about 15 years. At the turn of the century the lag will be only a decade.[1]

China's participation in international capital markets also is likely to continue to expand. Although the World Bank will reduce China's borrowing from the International Development Association (IDA), China is likely to remain the single largest borrower from the World Bank through the mid-1990s and to remain one of the largest borrowers from the Asian Development Bank.

Flows of official bilateral assistance are likely to grow, though not dramatically, beyond the record high level achieved in 1992. The sum of Chinese commercial borrowing, official export credits, and international bond sales also is likely to expand somewhat.

---

1. Adjusting to make the comparison in real rather than in nominal terms increases these lags by a year or two. But the essential point is little changed—China is quickly becoming a major world trader.

But of even greater importance as sources of foreign capital are the likely even larger inflows of foreign direct investment, the prospect of significantly increased portfolio investment by foreigners as China's equity markets expand, and the listing of more Chinese companies on foreign stock markets. Already by the end of 1993, China was probably the largest developing-country host of foreign investment.

Finally, China's role in the international economy will be enhanced further when the government formally makes its domestic currency convertible. As discussed in chapter 4, the *renminbi* by 1993 already was partially convertible for both current account and capital account transactions. In the 1980s China progressed significantly toward making its currency convertible. It reduced the degree of overvaluation of the official exchange rate and allowed a growing portion of export earnings to enter the swap market for foreign exchange, where market forces played a growing role in determining the value of the currency. But officials assiduously eschewed embracing convertibility as an eventual goal.

Pressures to move rapidly toward more complete convertibility grew in 1993. Most importantly, in the discussions of the Working Party on China's status in the General Agreement on Tariffs and Trade (GATT), the European Union made it clear that it regarded convertibility as a litmus test of China's successful progress toward a market economy. Largely as a result of this pressure, China changed its official policy on convertibility.

In 1992 and particularly in 1993, officials of the State Administration of Exchange Control, the Ministry of Foreign Trade and Economic Cooperation, and other relevant agencies repeatedly stated that China would move to a unified exchange rate within a year and move to convertibility within a few years. Similar assurances were presented to the GATT Working Party on China at its 14th meeting in May 1993.

At the end of 1993, China announced that, beginning in 1994, the dual exchange rate system would be replaced with a single unified official exchange rate that would be determined in the swap market. Even this partial step toward convertibility is likely to have a positive effect on inward foreign direct investment. In the recent past, foreign capital contributions in joint ventures were valued at the official exchange rate whereas domestic currency earnings converted to dollars for repatriation were converted at the swap rate. With the unification of the two rates, the previous price wedge, which imposed a high implicit tax on foreign partners in joint venture enterprises, disappears.

Will China Become a Global Economic Superpower?

In some quarters, China's rise as a major trading nation with significant participation in international capital markets is seen as a threat to the interests of the US and European Union. For example, according to press reports, the US Department of the Treasury predicted in late 1993 that by the end of the decade China would surpass Japan as the country with which the United States has its largest trade deficit ("U.S. Gamble with Beijing," *New York Times*, 17 November 1993, A1). Similarly, Gerald Segal (1993, 27) suggests that China's trade surpluses with the United States and the European Community "may well surpass those of Japan." Will China be an increasingly problematic participant in the international economic system? Will it become a low-wage, high-tech economy, with which even the most advanced industrial nations will find it difficult, if not impossible, to compete? Is it running a somewhat closed domestic market while running up large export surpluses, not only in North America but also in Europe?

An analysis of these issues logically begins with a review of some of the evidence presented in earlier chapters. The view that China will become an economic superpower stems in part from the widely pub-licized International Monetary Fund report that China's economy is poised to overtake that of Japan in absolute size and *The Economist*'s prediction, based on another study of China's real GDP, that China will be a larger economy than the United States shortly after the turn of the century. To begin with, many who read these reports quickly forget that China's population currently exceeds 1.1 billion and will grow by at least another several hundred million in coming decades, even if the regime is able to bring down the birth rate to a level that would lead to a stable population in the long run. What persisted in most memories was the idea that China would shortly be the largest economy in the world.

However, as argued in chapter 1, it seems much more likely that China's current per capita real output is about $1,000, not the much higher figure underlying the prediction cited above. Moreover, rather than simply extrapolating China's recent extraordinary growth experi-ence, it seems more reasonable to assume that much of the productivity-enhancing effects of economic reform will be exhausted by the turn of the century, and China's growth rate will diminish both absolutely and relative to that of other countries. Based on the assumptions laid out in chapter 1, the absolute size of the Chinese economy will not match that of the United States until 2040. And in per capita terms, China would not catch up to the United States for another century and a half, even if it could sustain a per capita growth rate twice that of the United States. In sum, China by virtue of its absolute size has become and will con-tinue to be a major participant in international trade and in international capital markets. But its per capita income is relatively low, and this will continue to be true for decades, even if the economy continues to do well.

If China will not become an economic superpower as conventionally defined, what about the fear that other nations, even advanced industrial economies, will not be able to compete with it? Doesn't its low income, and thus low wages, combined with an already high level of export earnings give it the capability to import advanced Western technology to create an invincible low-wage, high-tech economy?

The trade data analyzed in chapter 2 provide no support for this contention. If other countries cannot compete with China, how does one explain that in two out of three years since reform began in the late 1970s China has run a trade deficit? In almost all these years, China has run a current account deficit as well. The ability of foreign nations to sell more to China than it sells to them certainly does not support the vision of a China with which other nations, even advanced industrial nations, cannot compete.

Moreover, the evolving commodity composition of Chinese trade, also reviewed in chapter 2, suggests that China's trade is following a pattern increasingly consistent with the principle of comparative advantage. A key feature of trade based on comparative advantage is that all countries gain from participating in voluntary exchange and that their benefits from so doing will be even greater if over time they can shift a larger share of their labor and other productive factors into the sectors in which they enjoy a comparative advantage. In such a trading system, it will be less rational for high-income nations to produce large quantities of labor-intensive goods, such as low-quality garments, simple toys, and so forth. It makes more sense for high-income nations to provide the increasing levels of education and training that improve the quality of their labor forces and to shift these highly trained work forces increasingly into technologically more sophisticated industries.

The growing consistency of China's pattern of trade with comparative advantage is most obvious on the export side, where China supplies a growing share of the world's demand for relatively inexpensive garments and textiles and simple toys, footwear, and sporting goods. But the import side is equally revealing in this regard. The share of China's imports accounted for by industrial products has risen sharply and by 1993 accounted for almost nine-tenths of total imports. The fastest growing imports are of machinery and transportation equipment, particularly those embodying higher levels of technologies than China can produce domestically. In short, China is a growing market for the capital goods in which the most advanced industrial economies enjoy a comparative advantage. Thus, neither China's global trade balance nor the commodity composition of its trade provides any evidence that advanced industrial nations will lose their ability to compete with China.

What about the continually growing bilateral surplus China enjoys with the United States? Doesn't this suggest that China's economy is in some sense still closed? An analysis of this problem must begin with the explicit recognition that the bilateral US deficit with China, as recorded in US Department of Commerce data, almost certainly will expand significantly in the years immediately ahead. China is likely to remain the second largest deficit country for the United States, and if the real value of the yen remains at the high level attained in the third quarter of 1993, China could become the largest deficit trading partner of the United States. The reason is immediately apparent from an examination of table 4.1. In 1992 the ratio of US imports from China relative to US exports to China was almost 3.5-to-1. Thus simply to keep the trade deficit from widening, US exports to China would have to grow more than three times more rapidly than US imports from China. For example, if US exports to China continued to grow at the 20 percent rate of 1993 while imports from China grew only half as fast, by 1995 the US bilateral deficit would be $21.5 billion, one-sixth more than the $18.3 billion deficit of 1992.

This situation is similar to that the United States faced vis-à-vis Japan after the 1985 Plaza Agreement led to a substantial appreciation of the yen relative to the dollar. The appreciation of the yen contributed significantly to an acceleration of US exports to Japan relative to US imports from Japan. Indeed, between 1985 and 1992 US exports to Japan more than doubled while imports rose by only a third. Expressed on an annual basis, US exports rose at 11.0 percent per year while US imports rose at 4.3 percent per year. However, since the ratio of US imports from Japan relative to exports to Japan in 1985 was a little over 3-to-1, the absolute US bilateral trade deficit with Japan was unchanged. It stood at $49.8 billion in 1985 and $50.0 billion in 1992 (Bergsten and Noland 1993, 24–25).

Since the US trade imbalance with China, as measured by the ratio of US imports to US exports, stood at almost 3.5-to-1 in 1992, slightly greater than the proportional imbalance with Japan in 1985, the challenge of reducing the bilateral trade imbalance as recorded by the US Department of Commerce is even greater in the Chinese case. Since it is unlikely in the extreme that US exports to China will grow three and a half times more rapidly than its imports from China anytime soon, it seems virtually certain that the absolute bilateral imbalance with China, as measured by the United States, will widen significantly for several years. China's trade surplus may even surpass that of Japan over the next five to seven years, particularly if the relatively high real value the yen attained in the third quarter of 1993 persists, bringing Japan's surplus in its trade with the United States significantly below the record $59 billion level of 1993.

The widening US bilateral trade deficit already observed and likely to occur in the years ahead suggests that there may be certain parallels between the pattern of economic development of China and that of some other countries in East Asia, such as Japan, that lead to persistent and growing trade imbalances.

Is China a More Open Economy?

However, there are also fundamental differences that will perhaps be more important in the long term. One, already discussed in detail in chapter 2, is that China has run a systematic global trade and current account deficit since reform began. The few years of trade surplus since 1978 are explained largely by China's domestic macroeconomic cycle and its exchange rate policy. But, on average, China has run trade deficits (table 2.1). Since these deficits have been financed in part by external borrowing, its external debt has grown continuously since 1978 (table 3.1).

Second, I believe that in certain critical respects China is already somewhat more integrated into the world economy than Japan, Taiwan, or South Korea were at comparable stages of their economic development. By some measures, China is more open than these economies even on a contemporaneous basis. This greater integration gives China a stake in the evolution of the world economy that is potentially greater than that of Japan, Taiwan, or South Korea. This has important policy implications that will be discussed later in this chapter.

In what way does China have a deeper and more complex dependence on the world economy than Japan, Taiwan, or South Korea, either today or at comparable stages of their economic development? Obviously, China is not more open as measured by its trade ratio—that is, imports plus exports as a percentage of GNP. China is a huge continental economy with abundant natural resources and a domestic market sufficiently large to support a broad range of manufacturing industries. Thus, its need to import raw materials or to export in order to exploit scale economies in manufacturing is significantly less than even Japan, not to mention South Korea or Taiwan. In part for these reasons, China's estimated trade ratio of 9 percent in 1990, discussed in chapter 1, falls far below that of the countries just mentioned.

However, the economic openness of a country can be measured in other ways, such as the magnitude of inward foreign direct investment, the importance of foreign-invested firms in generating export earnings, the ability of domestic firms to access parts and components from abroad, the importance of the country as a source of outward foreign direct investment, or the openness of a country's equities markets to foreign investors.

The Magnitude of Foreign Investment in China

Foreign investment is more important in China than in most other countries in East Asia, though it is not necessarily more important than in some Southeast Asian countries, such as Thailand or Malaysia, where foreign investment plays a much greater role than in most of East Asia.

This greater relative importance of foreign investment in China is evident both in its magnitude and the role of foreign-invested firms in generating exports. The absolute magnitude of foreign investment in China, discussed in detail chapter 3, eclipses that in Japan, Taiwan, and Korea, both now and at comparable stages of their economic development. Estimates of cumulative foreign direct investment (FDI) in Japan through 1972 are subject to some uncertainty but range from $1.0 billion to as much as $3.4 billion (Krause and Sekiguchi 1976, 446). In nominal terms, even the higher estimate was less than 6 percent of the $60 billion cumulative foreign investment in China through the end of 1993 (table 3.7). Even taking into account price differences, there is little doubt that FDI in China dwarfed that in Japan during a comparable development period.

The reason is straightforward: the Japanese law on foreign investment, which dates to 1950, was extremely restrictive. Foreign ownership was limited to a maximum of 49 percent of any joint venture, and foreign investment was explicitly restricted in a large number of industries. Not until 1973 did the Japanese allow wholly foreign-owned firms to operate. Even to this day, Japan is far more restrictive than China with regard to investments in infrastructure and services. As a result, its total FDI stock is less than China's.

Similarly, China's foreign investment regime is far more liberal than that of South Korea. Despite some modest liberalization measures in the 1960s, South Korea's foreign investment regime throughout the 1970s was quite restrictive. Foreign ownership was limited to a maximum of 50 percent, and large numbers of sectors essentially were closed to foreign investment. Significant liberalization measures began only in the early 1980s. As a result, cumulative foreign investment in South Korea through 1981 was only $2.3 billion (SaKong 1993, 116–17). Indeed, the very recent liberalization of South Korea's foreign investment regime was stimulated partially by China. The South Korean government recognized that the decline in gross direct investment inflows in the early 1990s was due to the ability of China's increasingly liberal investment environment to attract foreign firms that otherwise would have invested in South Korea.

Although Taiwan was the beneficiary of substantial inflows of official US bilateral economic aid through 1965, the role of FDI was even less significant than in South Korea.

Dependence on Exports Produced by Foreign-Invested Firms

Not only is the magnitude of foreign investment in China greater, foreign-invested firms in China are playing a role in the growth of exports that has no parallel elsewhere in East Asia. As already discussed in chapter 3 and shown in table 3.9, the absolute value of exports and the share of China's total exports generated by foreign-invested firms grew steadily after the mid-1980s. In 1993 they totaled more than $25 billion and accounted for more than a fourth of all of China's exports. Foreign-funded exports were expected to grow by more than a third in 1994, which would further increase their share of China's total exports.

But these figures fail to capture the degree to which Chinese export growth is now dependent on foreign-invested firms. Exports of foreign-funded firms rose 45.4 percent in 1993 while China's total exports rose only 8 percent. As a result, foreign-invested firms accounted for seven-tenths of total export growth in 1993, surpassing their contribution in 1992, when they contributed three-fifths of incremental export growth.[2]

Foreign-invested firms in Japan and Taiwan never contributed more than a few percentage points of total exports. Only in South Korea did the share of exports produced by foreign-invested firms reach the two-digit level. Even so, this did not happen until 1984–86, at a relatively late stage of South Korea's economic development. Moreover, foreign-invested firms accounted for only 11 percent of South Korea's exports in those years, less than half the share in China in 1993 (SaKong 1993, 120).

The Importance of Processed Exports

The openness of China's economy is also evidenced by its liberal legal provisions facilitating exports based on processing or assembly activity (World Bank 1993a, 11). In 1984 China's State Council approved both "processing with supplied materials" and "processing with imported materials." In the first of these two schemes, sometimes called contract manufacturing, Chinese firms can bring in duty-free all materials and components supplied by foreign firms as part of export processing contracts. In this case, Chinese firms technically do not take ownership of the imported components and are paid a fee, on a per unit basis, for the assembly or processing activity. The value of these exports is the sum of the value of the imported components and the processing fee. International marketing is entirely in the hands of the foreign firm that supplies the materials and components. In the second scheme, Chinese firms import, free from customs duties, parts and components that are used to produce finished goods for export. The Chinese firms assume ownership of the components and are responsible for the sale of the final product on the world market.

As a result of the relatively smooth functioning of the duty exemption provisions of these laws, export processing is far more important in China than elsewhere in East Asia. Table 5.1 shows the growth after

---

2. Calculated based on data in tables 2.1 and 3.9.

Table 5.1   Industrial processing trade, 1985–91

Year	Imports		Exports	
	Millions of dollars	Percentage of total imports[a]	Millions of dollars	Percentage of total exports[a]
1985	1,974	4.7	2,368	8.7
1986	2,981	6.9	3,417	11.0
1987	4,874	11.3	4,740	12.0
1988	6,664	12.1	6,486	13.6
1989	7,002	11.8	8,230	15.7
1990	8,708	16.3	10,453	16.8
1991	10,934	17.1	12,925	18.0

a. These data include only processing based on materials supplied by foreign firms. Chinese firms also purchase their own raw materials and components that are used to produce processed exports.

Sources: Sung (1991b, 102); General Administration of Customs of the People's Republic of China.

1985 of imports supplied by foreign firms and the exports produced under the first of the two schemes described above. In 1991 these exports reached $12.925 billion, or 18 percent of all exports.

Processed exports produced under the second scheme have become even more important. In 1991, for example, these exports reached $19.5 billion, more than half again as much as the first type, and accounted for 27 percent of total exports (World Bank 1993a, 12).

Thus, in 1991 the combination of the two types of processed exports accounted for 45 percent of all exports. Since both types of processed exports are manufactured goods, it is interesting to note that in the same year processed exports accounted for almost three-fifths of all manufactured exports.[3] Put another way, the striking increase in manufactures as a share of China's total exports, discussed in chapter 2 and shown in table 2.2, is in large measure due to the growing importance of processed exports.[4]

3. Calculated based on total export and manufactured export data in tables 2.1 and 2.2.

4. One cannot simply add foreign-invested exports and processed exports to get some measure of the magnitude of total Chinese exports dependent on either foreign-invested firms or on imported foreign parts and components. The reason is that a significant share of the exports of foreign-invested firms are also processed exports, depending on imports of duty-free components and parts. Data on this are not published in any systematic fashion, but of $9.32 billion in exports of foreign-invested firms in the first half of 1993, $7.94 billion or 85.2 percent were processed exports (Zhao Cao 1993). The portion of processed exports in total exports has been rising. If we assume that the same is true for foreign-invested firms and that the proportion of processed exports in foreign-invested

By contrast, export processing was never significant in postwar Japan. Its share of exports of traditional labor-intensive products began to shrink as early as the second half of the 1950s because of rising labor costs.

Outward Foreign Direct Investment

Another way the Chinese economy is more open and linked to the international economy in more complex ways than were Japan, Taiwan, and South Korea at a comparable stage of economic development is in the magnitude of Chinese outward FDI. China does not publish data on outward investment, so its magnitude is uncertain. However, by 1993 it was commonly believed that cumulative Chinese investment in Hong Kong exceeded $10 billion. Although this was the single largest geographic concentration of FDI, China also had significant investments in many other countries. The World Bank (1993e, vol. 1, 51) estimates that in 1992 the flow of Chinese direct investment abroad reached $4 billion and that China had probably become the single largest source of outward FDI among developing countries.

Openness of Domestic Equities Markets

Finally, the Chinese economy is at least as open, and probably more open, than Japan, South Korea, and Taiwan as measured by the greater access foreigners have to domestic stock markets. Equity markets are in their infancy in China. But, if the appropriate regulatory structure can be developed, equity markets may grow rapidly in the years ahead. They possibly could play a much greater role in the mobilization of savings than was the case in Japan, South Korea, and Taiwan at comparable stages of development.

Of course, a greater role for equity markets, in and of itself, is not an indicator of openness. That depends on foreign access to and participation in these markets. China began to encourage foreign equity ownership in 1992, when it authorized companies listed on the Shanghai and Shenzhen exchanges to issue B shares for purchase by foreigners in hard

---

exports in 1991 was four-fifths, then we can estimate processed foreign-invested exports at $9.7 billion (four-fifths of the export value shown in table 3.9). That would leave $9.8 billion (in the total of $19.5 billion) as the value of processed exports under the second scheme of duty-free purchase of parts and components, with Chinese firms, as opposed to foreign-invested firms, doing the processing. Taking into account the hypothesized one-fifth of exports of foreign-invested firms in 1991 that were not processed exports, the sum of processed and joint venture exports that year can be estimated as $34.87 billion, or 49 percent of all exports and 63 percent of all manufactured exports.

currency.[5] By mid-1993 foreign holdings accounted for 5 percent of the combined capitalization on the two markets.

By comparison, Japan, Korea, and Taiwan did not begin to open their equity markets until quite recently and in each case only as a result of lengthy bilateral negotiations with the US government. The US government is continuing negotiations with these countries in an attempt to move beyond the initial cautious opening measures.

Korea did not open its equity market to foreign investors until 1992 and limits foreign ownership to a maximum of 10 percent of each issue. Taiwan has allowed foreign participation in its equity markets only since 1991, but it remains perhaps the least open equity market in Asia. It imposes extensive regulations on foreign shareholders, including repatriation restrictions that don't exist in China. Toward the end of 1993, only about 1 percent of Taiwan's market capitalization was in foreign hands, significantly less than on the mainland.

China in 1993 also sold seats on both the Shanghai and Shenzhen securities markets to foreign stockbrokers. Although the number of foreign seats is less than would be desirable, the initial sale was substantially earlier than was the case in Japan, Taiwan, or Korea.

Implications

The relative openness of the Chinese economy has important implications for the likely evolution of China's global trade balance and for bilateral balances with individual countries. As much as 40 percent of world trade is now intrafirm. This trade between parent companies and their subsidiaries abroad in turn has a significant effect on patterns of trade. In the common phrase, trade follows investment. In 1988, for example, two-fifths of US imports and over a third of US exports were accounted for by US multinationals trading with firms abroad in which they had some form of investment (Encarnation 1992, 28).

Japan's relatively inhospitable foreign investment environment is widely believed to be a factor contributing to Japan's global trade surplus and its bilateral surplus with the United States. US firms have invested relatively little in Japan. Thus they ship relatively modest amounts of machinery and equipment to joint ventures in Japan, and their shipments of parts and components to Japan are similarly limited.

On the other hand, Japanese multinationals take advantage of the relatively open investment environment in the United States and in Southeast Asia. By the end of 1991 they had invested six times more in the United States than American multinationals had invested in Japan (Bergsten and Noland 1993, 80).

---

5. The B shares are actually listed on these markets in terms of *renminbi*, but their purchase by foreigners must be in hard currency.

These investment flows affect trade flows. For example, beginning in the mid-1980s, after the Plaza Agreement led to a prolonged period of yen appreciation, Japanese corporations began to invest heavily in Southeast Asia. Japanese firms shifted production of consumer electronics and other relatively labor-intensive manufactures to affiliate companies in Southeast Asia. Although most of this production was sold in third countries, some Japanese companies began to import these products back into Japan. But Japan's trade surplus with Southeast Asian countries actually rose because the Japanese sale of production machinery and of technologically advanced, high valued-added components to their foreign affiliates in Southeast Asia more than offset the increased imports of finished goods from Southeast Asia to Japan.

If the same pattern holds with respect to China, it would appear unlikely that China will soon run a global balance of payments surplus. The huge flow of foreign direct investment into China, for example, is largely realized in the form of machinery and equipment supplied by foreign participants in joint ventures. In China's trade accounts, these are counted as imports. Once joint venture and wholly foreign-owned plants are up and running, there is a continual flow of parts and components from the parent firm abroad to the joint venture company in China. About four-fifths of all joint venture exports are produced with imported parts and components (footnote 4).

As discussed in chapter 3 and earlier in this chapter, joint venture firms located in China have become major exporters. However, the imports of these firms, including the machinery and equipment that forms part of their initial capitalization, as well as parts and components used in production, in recent years have exceeded their exports by a wide margin. For example, in 1993 foreign-funded enterprises were net importers to the tune of $16.6 billion.[6] Machinery and equipment imports attributable to joint ventures will rise sharply in 1994, probably more than offsetting the expected one-third increase in joint venture exports. Thus, as long as foreign direct investment expands rapidly, the overall influence of inward FDI will continue to be to push China's trade account into deficit.[7]

---

6. In 1993, imports attributable to foreign-funded firms in China, including machinery and equipment brought in as part of the foreign participant's capital contribution as well as parts and components, were $41.83 billion. Exports of products produced by these foreign-funded firms were $25.24 billion ("China's Foreign Trade Increase to Reach $195.7 Billion," *People's Daily*, 10 January 1994).

7. Of course, the deficit of foreign-funded enterprises is not likely to continue indefinitely. When the rate of inflow of new FDI declines relative to the stock of previous investment, it is likely that the foreign-invested sector will become a net exporter. The degree to which this becomes true will depend on the relative portions of the output of joint venture firms sold on domestic and international markets, respectively.

Implications for the United States

In recent years the growth of demand for US exports has accounted for fully half the expansion of the US economy. Developing-country markets have become increasingly important sources of this export demand. In 1991 and 1992, for example, US exports to developing countries grew by 15.2 and 13.7 percent, respectively. By contrast, exports to developed-country markets expanded by only 2.6 and 1.8 percent, respectively, in those years. Since developing-country markets are relatively important, equal to more than three-fifths of US sales to developed countries, the increment of US export sales to developing-country markets has been several times that to developed-country markets in recent years. For example, in 1992 US exports to developing countries grew by more than $20 billion, more than four times the incremental growth in exports of $4.6 billion to developed countries.[8]

Among the developing countries, China has emerged as the fastest growing large market for US firms. Although media attention in the United States has been focused on the bilateral deficit, US exports to China grew 54 percent in 1991 and 1992 and expanded by a further 21.5 percent in the first three quarters of 1993. In 1992 alone, US exports to China grew almost 20 percent, more than 10 times the average rate of growth of US exports to developed-country markets and almost half again as rapidly as the average growth of US exports to all developing countries. As a result of this relatively rapid growth, by 1992 China was the sixth largest developing-country market for US exporters.

The growth of exports to the six largest developing-country markets of the United States in 1991–93 is shown in figure 5.1. Over this period, US exports to China grew far more rapidly than those to any other major developing-country market. Indeed, the cumulative rate of expansion of US exports to China over this period is roughly twice that to Mexico, Taiwan, Singapore, or Hong Kong.

And the analysis immediately above understates China's importance as a trading partner and the growth of US exports to this market because it is based on US Department of Commerce data. As discussed in chapter 4, these data do not reflect US goods reexported to China from Hong Kong. As shown in table 4.2a, these indirect exports have been growing more rapidly than direct exports and reached almost $2.5 billion in 1992. If these goods are treated as exports to China, as they should be, China in 1992 ranked ahead of Hong Kong as the fifth largest developing-

---

8. The great importance of developing-country markets as sources of incremental exports in 1991–92 in part reflects slow economic growth in Europe and Japan in those years relative to Asia, where five of the six most rapidly growing US export markets in 1991–93 were located (figure 5.1). When European and Japanese recovery get under way, one can anticipate that the share of incremental US exports going to developed-country markets will rise.

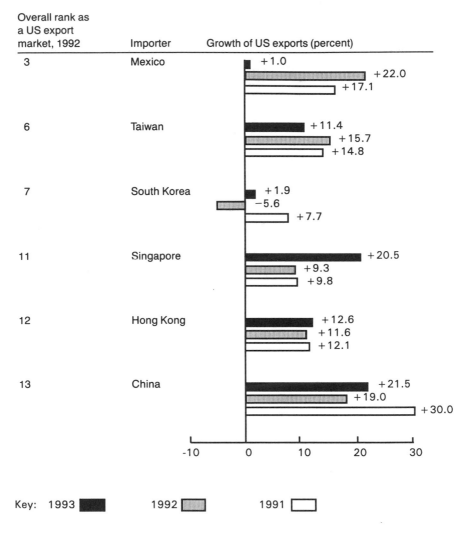

Figure 5.1 Growth of US exports to major developing country markets, 1991-93

Overall rank as
a US export
market, 1992 — Importer — Growth of US exports (percent)

3	Mexico	+1.0 / +22.0 / +17.1
6	Taiwan	+11.4 / +15.7 / +14.8
7	South Korea	+1.9 / −5.6 / +7.7
11	Singapore	+20.5 / +9.3 / +9.8
12	Hong Kong	+12.6 / +11.6 / +12.1
13	China	+21.5 / +19.0 / +30.0

Key: 1993 ■   1992 ▦   1991 ☐

Source: US Department of Commerce. Data for 1993 are the growth of exports through September compared to the first nine months of 1992.

country export market of the United States. And US exports to China in 1991–92 grew by 59 percent rather than the 54 percent figure mentioned earlier, which was based on the Department of Commerce data.

Similarly, US direct investment in China, although small, is increasing. Contracts for foreign investment in China signed by US firms in 1992 reached more than $3 billion, an almost fivefold increase over the

Table 5.2 United States: foreign direct investment in China, 1983–93 (millions of dollars)

Year	Contracted	Actual
1983	477.52	n.a.
1984	165.18	256.25
1985	1,152.02	357.19
1986	527.35	314.90
1987	432.19	262.80
1988	235.96	235.96
1989	640.52	284.27
1990	357.82	455.99
1991	548.08	323.20
1992	3,121.25	511.05
1993[a]	n.a.	280.00

n.a. = not available

a. First half of the year.

Sources: Ministry of Foreign Economic Relations and Trade, *Almanac of China's Foreign Economic Relations and Trade*, various years; Zhao Cao (1993).

previous year (table 5.2). Actual investment, which follows with a lag, rose almost 60 percent in 1992. In the first half of 1993, actual investment was $280 million, double that of the same period in 1992.

The Japanese Challenge

While China is an increasingly important export market and a destination for growing investment by US firms, in recent years Japan has become far more successful in exploiting China's emerging market. In part, this is because the Japanese government provides more support for trade with and investment in China for its firms than does the US government for US firms.

This growing disparity was evident even before Tiananmen but became more obvious in its aftermath. In 1989 Japan and other advanced industrial states applied sanctions against China that were similar to those of the United States. As has already been suggested in chapter 3 and will be discussed in detail below, within a year of Tiananmen, US policy vis-à-vis China increasingly diverged from both that of Japan and major industrial countries in Europe. Japan began marking out its own independent policy vis-à-vis China at the Houston G-7 summit in July 1990, where Prime Minister Toshiki Kaifu informed the leaders of the world's major industrial nations that Japan was planning to approve new bilateral loans for China under its third yen loan package covering 1990–95 and lift other restrictions on economic relations with Beijing. Several months prior to the G-7 meeting, Japan and China already had begun preparatory talks on the resumption of bilateral aid, and Japanese experts had been hard at work completing the required feasibility studies so that the projects could be initiated shortly after the new loans were approved.

Initially the Japanese moved slowly, approving ¥120 billion ($80 million) in new projects financed by the third Overseas Economic Cooperation Fund (OECF) loan package in the fall of 1990. Subsequently the Japanese stepped up the pace of loan approvals. As a result, by the end of 1993 they had approved about $5 billion in loans for specific projects, about three-fourths of the funds promised in the third yen loan package.

Most Japanese aid is nominally untied. This may seem surprising since in the mid-1970s over half of all aid was officially tied, but by 1990 none was. Similarly, OECD data, which are calculated on a different basis, show that Japan's share of tied aid is among the lowest of the major donors (Ensign 1992, 16–17). In reality, however, the number of non-Japanese companies that have won procurement contracts for OECF financed projects in recent years is extraordinarily small. Over 1986–90, only 14 non-Japanese companies bid successfully on these projects, and the share of foreign procurement was less than 10 percent of the total. Thus the loan component of Japanese aid is effectively tied to purchases from Japan (Ensign 1992, 50 and 63).

As already noted in chapter 3, Japanese aid is concentrated in basic infrastructure projects in the telecommunications, transportation, and energy sectors rather than in rural development or basic human needs projects. Since assistance in these sectors requires a high level of imported capital goods, Japan's aid program provides substantial assistance to its own export-oriented industries.

The challenge posed by Japanese and European development assistance to US firms attempting to sell in China is acute. Even before Tiananmen, the United States was the only industrialized country without a concessional loan or mixed credit program for China. US programs to promote US trade with and investment in China have been limited to three very modest programs: lending and loan guarantees through the US Export-Import Bank (Eximbank); investment guarantees by the Overseas Private Investment Corporation (OPIC), a US government agency, for firms investing in China; and technical assistance through the Trade and Development Program (TDP) administered by the US Agency for International Development (Harding 1992, 150).[9]

Even these are not all correctly referred to as assistance since, for example, guarantees of US investment involve no transfer of resources

9. This program is now called the Trade and Development Agency (TDA).

to the Chinese but simply reduce the risk of private investment committed to China. Only in the event of an expropriation of the assets of US firms by the Chinese government would the OPIC program provide a transfer to China. Similarly, loan guarantees by the US Eximbank do not normally entail a transfer to the Chinese. Unless the Chinese default on the loans and the commercial lender collects from the Export-Import Bank, no transfer of funds is involved.[10] Even regular Eximbank loans have a modest grant component since interest rates are not much below market. Loans authorized in 1992 carried rates that ranged from a low of 7.12 percent to a high of 7.95 percent. Only in the case of Eximbank grants is there an explicit subsidy. These grants, by law, are combined with loan funds provided by commercial banks, resulting in a so-called mixed-credit loan with a below-market interest rate. Since 1989 the Eximbank has authorized only one grant for China (discussed below).

TDP is more complex. It provides grants to US firms to do feasibility studies on potential projects in China with the expectation that the specifications for the project will lead to orders for machinery and equipment or other components supplied by US firms, including the firm conducting the feasibility study. No direct transfer of funds to the Chinese is involved.

In any case, the resources committed to these programs have been very small. Through the end of 1988, cumulative authorized Eximbank financing for trade with China was $349 million, of which only a portion had been disbursed; guarantees of direct investment by US firms in China by OPIC were a very modest $95.5 million; and cumulative TDP commitments for feasibility studies in China were only $22.6 million (Harding 1992, 150).

By contrast, over the same period Japanese Eximbank financing that was actually disbursed for trade with China was $1,984.5 million, or more than five times that authorized by the US Eximbank. Japan's International Cooperation Agency provides funding for feasibility studies, but its annual worldwide budget just prior to Tiananmen was 20 times that of the US TDP. The differential has widened since. Its budget is now more than $1 billion whereas the annual TDA budget is $30 million to $40 million (Preeg 1993, 113).[11]

---

10. Although they entail no direct transfer to the Chinese in most circumstances, both OPIC investment guarantees and Eximbank loans now do involve a budgetary cost. Under the terms of the Federal Credit Reform Act of 1990, which took effect at the beginning of the 1992 fiscal year, US agencies, such as the Eximbank, are required to estimate the total future costs of each of its transactions. These estimates are critically dependent on the assessment of the creditworthiness of the country that is the recipient of each loan, grant, or guarantee. Credit and other activities for riskier countries entail a higher estimated cost and thus absorb a larger share of the total amount of funds appropriated annually by the Congress for the particular activity (General Accounting Office 1993b, 5–6).

11. This was previously known as the Trade and Development Program (TDP).

Even these modest US programs in support of trade with and investment in China were suspended shortly after 4 June 1989. The International Development and Finance Act of 1989 suspended all Eximbank
loans to China and canceled both the TDP and OPIC programs in China.
The legislation did provide for a resumption of Eximbank lending to
China on a case-by-case basis if the US president certified that a specific
loan was in the "national interest." The president issued such a waiver
on 19 December 1989, and in early February 1990 the Eximbank
approved a $9.75 million loan to the China National Offshore Oil Corpo-
ration to finance engineering services for a gas processing plant. A few
days later, the Bank announced it had approved loan guarantees and
grants totaling $23.2 million for US signaling and other equipment for a
Shanghai subway project. In both cases the waivers of the sanctions
were justified on the basis that the US firms would lose the business to
foreign firms if the Eximbank credit was not made available. But fiscal
1990 authorizations for China of $37.5 million were only one-fourth
those in the year ending September 1989 (table 5.3). New authorizations
in fiscal 1991 were even less, only $35 million. In fiscal 1991 China was
not even among the top 10 recipients of US Eximbank financing. Not
until fiscal 1992, when authorizations totaled a little over $400 million,
did the level of activity surpass the pre-Tiananmen level. But the total
authorization figure for 1992 is somewhat misleading since it is not
comparable with earlier years. The main reason authorizations rose so
sharply in 1992 was a jump in credit guarantees from $20 million in 1991
to $330 million in 1992. The large increase in guarantees in 1992 was for
loans taken out by China Eastern Airlines to purchase two MD-11 air-
liners. Direct loans authorized for China by the US Eximbank in 1992
were less than half those of 1989.

The US Eximbank program looks even smaller when measured by
loan disbursements. These have not exceeded $100 million annually
since Tiananmen (table 5.3). These numbers pale when compared with
the actual disbursements of official Japanese export credits (table 3.5b).
Japanese disbursements in 1990 and 1991 were more than seven times
those of the United States.

The combined effect of Japan's growing support for its bilateral economic relationship with China and the diminished support of the US
government for the same is reflected in the figures on the evolving
bilateral trade and investment relations between the two pairs of countries. In short, Japanese firms appear to be doing very much better on
both trade with and investment in China.

The result of Japan's growing support for its bilateral trade with China
is reflected in the extraordinarily fast-growing trade flows between the
two countries. Japan's exports to China by 1992 almost doubled compared with 1990 (table 5.4), substantially ahead of the 54 percent
increase in US exports to China. That trend accelerated in the first half of

Table 5.3   United States: Export-Import Bank lending to China, 1989–92 (millions of dollars)

Fiscal year	Total authorizations[a]	Loan disbursements[b]
1989	147.660	49.0
1990	37.509	83.0
1991	35.107	83.0
1992	402.749	

a. Authorizations are the sum of loans, grants, and loan guarantees.

b. Loan disbursements are exclusive of funds extended by commercial banks that are guaranteed by the Export-Import Bank.

Sources: Export-Import Bank of the United States, Annual Report, various issues; Organization for Economic Cooperation and Development, Geographic Distribution of Financial Flows to Developing Countries, various years.

Table 5.4   Japan: trade with China, 1985–93[a] (millions of dollars)

Year	Exports	Imports	Balance
1985	12,477	6,483	+5,994
1986	9,856	5,653	+4,203
1987	8,250	7,401	+849
1988	9,476	9,859	−382
1989	8,516	11,146	−2,630
1990	6,130	12,054	−5,924
1991	8,593	14,216	−5,623
1992	11,949	16,953	−5,004
1993[b]	7,827	8,771	−944

a. Customs clearance statistics of the Japanese Ministry of Finance.

b. First half of the year.

Source: Japan External Trade Organization, China Newsletter, various issues.

1993, when Japan's exports to China grew by more than 50 percent compared with the first half of the previous year. By comparison, US exports to China grew by about a fifth over the same period. Thus, although US exports to China have been growing rapidly since 1990, the average annual growth of Japanese exports to China was even more rapid, actually several times the growth of US exports to China.

On the other hand, Japanese imports from China, while up sharply, have not increased as rapidly as its exports. As a result, the record $5.9 billion deficit Japan recorded in its trade with China in 1990 dropped to under a billion dollars in the first half of 1993. The contrast with the rapidly rising US bilateral trade deficit with China over the same period is obvious.

Bilateral Sino-Japanese trade is developing so rapidly that in 1993 China became Japan's second largest trading partner, compared with fifth largest in 1992. In so doing, China surpassed Germany, Taiwan, and South Korea in importance as trading partners of Japan. The gains were largely in Japanese exports since in 1992 China was already the second largest supplier of imports to Japan, a rank it retained in 1993.

A comparative analysis shows that Japanese firms also have over-taken the United States as a source of foreign investment in China. Foreign direct investment by Japanese firms in China has increased markedly in recent years (table 5.5). A comparison with the data in table 5.2 shows that through 1987 annual FDI in China by US firms exceeded that of Japanese firms. Starting in 1988 the annual flow of Japanese direct investment moved ahead of that of the United States. In the early 1990s, cumulative Japanese investment in China exceeded that of the United States for the first time, making Japan the third largest investor in China after Hong Kong and Taiwan. The United States, long in second place in cumulative investment, slipped to fourth. The differential in annual FDI flows widened in the first half of 1993. Japanese firms invested $610 million, almost triple the amount for the same period in 1992. US firms invested $280 million, double the amount in the first half of 1992 but less than half of the Japanese amount (Zhao Cao 1993).[12]

Recommendations for US Policy

President Clinton often has said that economics is the central focus of his foreign policy and that Asia is the most rapidly growing portion of the world economy, offering the greatest potential for the expansion of US exports and the creation of new jobs in the United States. In short, trade expansion is the foundation of a strategy to reinvigorate US growth and increase US competitiveness in global markets, and Asia offers more trade opportunities than any other part of the globe.

In certain respects, US policy toward China is consistent with these objectives. The September 1993 decision to modify substantially the controls on the export of computers and telecommunications equipment, for example, is anticipated by the Clinton administration to lead to an additional $35 billion in annual international sales of these items on a

---

12. Based on contracts signed, US firms seem to be doing better than their Japanese counterparts. In 1992 there was a fivefold increase in the value of investment contracts signed by US firms compared with 1991, while contracts signed by Japanese firms increased less than twofold. Moreover, the value of contracts signed by US firms was almost half again as large as the value of contracts signed by Japanese firms. The analysis in the text is based on actual investment rather than contracts signed because Japanese firms are very cautious in signing contracts for investment in China. The Chinese report that the ratio of realized investment to contracted investment is higher for Japanese companies than that of any other country.

Table 5.5 Japan: foreign direct investment in China, 1983–93 (millions of dollars)

Year	Contracted	Actual
1983	94.50	n.a.
1984	203.04	224.58
1985	470.68	315.07
1986	210.42	201.33
1987	301.36	219.70
1988	275.79	514.53
1989	438.61	356.34
1990	457.00	503.38
1991	812.20	532.50
1992	2,172.53	709.83
1993[a]	n.a.	610.00

n.a. = not available

a. First half of the year.

Sources: Ministry of Foreign Economic Relations and Trade, *Almanac of China's Foreign Economic Relations and Trade*, various years; Zhao Cao (1993).

worldwide basis. US exporters of these goods to China will benefit from these changes. The decision also fulfills one of the three commitments the United States made in the bilateral market access agreement of 1992 to liberalize the export restrictions that limit Chinese access to advanced technology. The September decision was followed in December 1993 by a preliminary ruling of the Department of Commerce that should ulti-mately (but which had not as of mid-January, as will be discussed below) allow the sale of advanced fiber-optic communications equipment spe-cifically to China and the former Soviet Union. When finalized, this decision, too, will fulfill one of the commitments the United States made in the market-access memorandum of understanding. Similarly, as men-tioned in chapter 4, the Clinton administration approved the sale of a Cray supercomputer in late 1993. In early January 1994 it approved the sale to China of two satellites built by Martin Marietta Corporation. And in early March 1994 it announced it would approve the sale of an addi-tional satellite made by Hughes Aircraft Company. These actions par-tially lifted the Missile Technology Control Regime (MTCR) sanctions it had imposed in August 1993. Finally, though it was at least temporarily blocked by Japan and the Europeans, in early 1994 the administration sought to further ease the COCOM limits on computer exports.

The Clinton administration in the fall of 1993 also approved a policy of higher level engagement between American and Chinese government officials. That led to a series of visits to China by high-level US government officials. The first visit was by John Shattuck, assistant secretary of state for human rights. US Treasury Secretary Lloyd Bentsen visited China in January 1994. This sequence of high-level visits culminated in a trip by US Secretary of State Warren Christopher in mid-March. Bentsen's visit provided the occasion for reviving the Joint Economic Commission. The JEC, co-chaired by the US treasury secretary and the Chinese minister of finance, had met annually until 1989 to address a range of important bilateral issues in finance, banking, and taxation. In the first formal meeting since the suspension of the bilateral talks, the American side apparently agreed to provide the Chinese technical advice to assist them in the use of modern tools of macroeconomic management to sustain noninflationary economic growth. In the revival of the JEC talks, the United States also agreed that the US Federal Reserve Board chairman and officials of the US Internal Revenue Service and the Securities and Exchange Commission would visit China to provide assistance on monetary policy, tax issues, and securities regulation, respectively.

These liberalizations on the sale of US technology to China and the restoration of cabinet-level contacts are positive developments that are consistent with the president's expressed wish to further engage the United States in the most rapidly growing region of the world economy. On the other hand, the executive order that extended China's most-favored nation (MFN) status in the US market through 2 July 1994 stated that China's MFN status would not be extended again unless China made overall, significant progress in the area of human rights. Specific factors listed include respecting the fundamental human rights recognized in the Universal Declaration of Human Rights; allowing freedom to emigrate and travel abroad; providing an accounting of and releasing those imprisoned for the peaceful expression of their political views; ending forced abortions and sterilizations as instruments of China's family planning policies; ceasing religious persecution; ensuring that prisoners are not mistreated and have access to medical care; protecting Tibet's religious and cultural heritage and resuming a dialogue with the Dalai Lama or his representatives; and ending the jamming of Voice of America broadcasts (White House press release 28 May 1993, 5). In short, the executive order extending China's MFN status links the continuation of that status very closely to a long list of human rights considerations.

US policy toward China should be structured not only in response to evolving human rights conditions in China but with three additional key facts in mind. First, as already discussed in the closing section of chapter 4, discontinuation of China's MFN status in the US market would substantially dislocate trade flows between China and the United States and might well initiate an overall downward spiral in bilateral relations. Because the costs of MFN discontinuation would be so high and because they would fall to a considerable degree on US firms, discontinuation of China's MFN status should be considered only as a policy instrument of last resort when other alternatives have been exhausted.

Second, in some respects China is one of the more open economies in Asia. Not surprisingly, like other developing economies, China seeks to continue to protect a broad range of domestic manufacturing industries from the full brunt of international competition. But on balance, its economy is more open than that of other East Asian economies at comparable stages of economic development and in certain respects is even more open than they are now. US policy should seek to encourage and further this openness by more fully engaging China in the world economy. Multilaterally, that means bringing China under the disciplines of the General Agreement on Tariffs and Trade (GATT) as soon as possible. Bilaterally, that means working to provide China more certain access to the US market by granting permanent MFN status as soon as sufficient evidence accumulates that China is in compliance with the terms specified in the protocol governing its participation in the GATT.

Third, China will be an increasingly important source of growth, to some degree for the world economy, and certainly even more so in Asia. Already China is the second largest trading country in Asia. Its rapidly growing imports are increasingly important for generating domestic economic growth not only in Hong Kong, but increasingly in Taiwan and even in Japan. The result is that in 1993, for the first time ever, more goods produced in Hong Kong were sold to China than to the United States, traditionally Hong Kong's largest export market. Taiwan enjoys booming trade and a huge bilateral surplus as the mainland quickly emerges as the most rapidly growing export market for the island. Even in Japan, certain industries such as steel and automobiles have become increasingly dependent on the Chinese market.

The challenge for the United States is to craft a policy that both facilitates US economic interaction with this most rapidly growing part of the world economy and also advances other objectives, such as human rights and nonproliferation. Inevitably, there is some tension between these objectives, particularly in the short run. However, US policy should take a long-term perspective.

Indeed, key US policy objectives with respect to China are most likely to be complementary in the long run. If the United States remains at loggerheads with China on a long list of bilateral economic issues including market access, intellectual property protection, prison labor, and textiles, the Chinese government may be less, not more, likely to improve human rights conditions, comply with the terms of the MTCR, and cooperate in controlling the spread of nuclear weapons on the Korean peninsula. In short, if the economic relationship deteriorates, China may have less of an incentive to work cooperatively on noneconomic issues.

On the other hand, the further engagement of China would give the regime an even greater stake in the international economy, encouraging it to take steps on noneconomic issues that it would not likely take if its global economic participation was diminishing.

At the same time, the further engagement of China in the world economy over time almost certainly will accelerate the domestic transformations that are most likely to lead to a more pluralistic political system and ultimately a more favorable human rights environment. Recent experience in East Asia suggests that an economy that is successful in using the market to allocate goods and services eventually will stimulate a demand for comparable choices in governance and political leadership. Economic sanctions against China, both actual and threatened, are likely to diminish the influence within the country of those Chinese supporting reform, retard the further engagement of China in the world economy, inhibit the deepening reliance on the use of the market to allocate resources in its domestic economy, and thus also delay the pressures for political choice that matches the choice existing in the economic sphere.

US objectives in Asia are most likely to be accomplished by treating China as a strategic partner rather than a backlash state, as President Clinton's national security adviser labeled it (Anthony Lake, speech at Johns Hopkins University School of Advanced International Studies, 21 September 1993). The United States, for example, envisages the Asia Pacific Economic Cooperation (APEC) forum as a key component of its long-run strategy to strengthen US regional trading ties and to promote broader economic cooperation among economies of the region. Yet it will be difficult for the United States to achieve this objective if it is the only economy in the region that uses unilateral economic sanctions rather than regional cooperation to promote human rights and achieve other objectives.

The specific recommendations that follow would go a long way toward realizing the objective of treating China as a more equal partner rather than a backlash state that is expected to cave in to unilaterally imposed US sanctions.

- Abandon use of the bilateral trade imbalance as an indicator of the degree of openness of the Chinese economy or the state of Sino-American relations.

- Provide export credits to American firms seeking to sell in China that are comparable to those provided to European and Japanese firms by their governments.

- Revise US export controls to make them maximally multilateral, eliminating unilateral export prohibitions whenever alternative uncontrolled sources of supply are available.

- Revise the multilateral organizations designed to limit the spread of weapons of mass destruction (the MTCR, the Nuclear Suppliers Group, or NSG, and the Australia Group, or AG) to provide meaningful multilateral sanctions in the event of violations, thus eliminating US unilateral sanctions.

- Work for China's early entry into the GATT, preferably before the end of 1994.

- Seek to provide China permanent MFN status in the United States conditional upon evidence that China is in compliance with the protocol governing its participation in the GATT.

- Drop charges of Chinese currency manipulation until evidence warrants them.

- Continue to expand US cabinet-level contacts with Chinese ministerial counterparts and enhance the role of formal bilateral commissions such as the Joint Economic Commission and the US-China Joint Commission on Commerce and Trade (JCCT).

The Bilateral Trade Imbalance

The United States should abandon using the bilateral imbalance in its trade with China as a meaningful measure or indicator of either the degree of openness of the Chinese economy or of the state of Sino-American relations. The US Treasury Department in particular has pointed to the bilateral deficit as a matter of serious concern. Continual comparisons of the size of the bilateral deficit that the United States has with China, on the one hand, and Japan, on the other, obscure the fact that the two countries are fundamentally different. Japan's global trade surplus rose continuously over the decade ending in 1993 whereas China, on average, has incurred trade and current account deficits and thus has cumulated a significant external debt.

One underlying reason US policy thinking on this point is confused is China's unique trade position. In recent decades, China is the only country with which the United States has run a significant deficit that has *not* been a global surplus country as well. Japan is the obvious contrast, a point already made. But Taiwan, Korea, Canada, and Germany, among others, also ran large global trade surpluses in the years when their bilateral surpluses with the United States were significant. Taiwan, from the mid-1980s onward, when it was running a large surplus in its trade with the United States, for example, also had a global surplus that was one of the largest in the world. South Korea also followed this pattern. Beginning in the mid-1980s, the surplus in its trade with the United States was among the largest. And it had a large global trade surplus from 1986 through 1989. As its global trade balance shrank in 1990 and then went into deficit in 1991, its bilateral surplus with the United States fell dramatically. By 1992 it did not even rank among the top 10 deficit trading partners of the United States.

A full explanation of the causes of China's unique trade position vis-à-vis the United States lies beyond the scope of this study. But among the factors that appear most relevant are US export disincentives, discussed further below. Richardson (1993) estimated that, in the absence of national security controls that are more stringent than those of other advanced industrial countries and with official support for export finance comparable to its global competitors, US exports to China in 1989 would have been $5 billion to $10 billion higher. Since in the same year the officially reported US deficit was $6.2 billion (table 4.1) and the estimated adjusted deficit was less than $4 billion (table 4.2), it would appear that at least in 1989 the US deficit was almost entirely explained by US policies.

Since 1989 the US deficit, both as reported by the Department of Commerce (table 4.1) and on an adjusted basis (table 4.2), has tripled. But US export disincentives have grown as well for three reasons. First, the relative impact of US sanctions on trade with China also has grown. This is partly because China's other trading partners all have eliminated the economic sanctions they imposed in 1989. Thus what was initially a regime of multilateral sanctions has become a regime of unilateral trade sanctions. And the scope of the sanctions has expanded, as the United States has been the only country to impose any sanctions on China under the provisions of the MTCR.

Second, beginning in 1990 the uncertainty effect of the annual MFN renewal has become a significant factor for the first time, serving as a powerful but difficult-to-measure disincentive, not only for exports to China but also for US foreign direct investment in China. This was not a factor in earlier years because, as noted in chapter 4, annual renewal of China's MFN trade status in the US market was routine in the 1980s. Although the discontinuation of China's MFN status, in the first instance, would reduce Chinese exports to the United States, Chinese retaliation would impose costs on US exporters and possibly US investors in China as well. These potential costs must be weighed by any company considering either the initial development or the expansion of existing sales into the China market or investing to establish a joint venture in China. Again, because the United States is the only country that requires an annual renewal of China's MFN status, this uncertainty applies only to US trade with and investment in China.

Third, other countries have increased their concessional loan and export credit commitments to China while the United States remains the only major industrial country without a program of bilateral economic assistance to China and offers export credits that are very small compared with its competitors. The salience of this factor is accentuated by the growing importance in China of major infrastructure projects in telecommunications, transportation, and electric power generation. Given the capital intensity of these projects and their long gestation periods, concessional finance and/or export credits are an unusually effective sales tool of Japanese and European firms.

US policy toward China seemingly ignores these factors that contribute to China's unique combination of a global trade deficit and a bilateral surplus in trade with the United States. Rather than recognizing the importance of factors that are directly or indirectly controlled by US policy, the US government in its bilateral discussions with the Chinese implicitly assumes that the bilateral deficit is largely the result of an insufficiently open Chinese market. In many respects, the market opening policies that the United States is pursuing vis-à-vis China replicate those currently pursued vis-à-vis Japan or in the past with Taiwan and South Korea. There is some rationale for discussing market opening measures, including more expansionary fiscal policies to stimulate growth and thus imports as well, when these countries run large global surpluses. But it makes little sense to argue, as senior US policymakers did several times in the latter half of 1993, that the Chinese market was closed when China was running a large trade and current account deficit. This is not to say that China lacks sector-specific import barriers that should be the focus of bilateral negotiations. But the elimination of such barriers would most likely result in a change in the composition of Chinese imports rather than an increase in the level of total imports.

Rather than focusing on the bilateral deficit and pursuing market opening measures that may be more appropriate to global surplus countries, the US objective should be to seek a commitment from China to avoid a position of systematic global trade surplus in the future. For reasons explained above, I believe that China is likely to be a net borrower over the mid-term, meaning China will incur current account deficits on average. Looking further ahead, however, these deficits need not continue indefinitely, particularly if China succeeds in sustaining the relatively high rates of domestic saving that have been evident in recent years. China need not be a net borrower indefinitely to sustain high rates of investment. Thus at some point in the future, China could combine current account surpluses with significant net capital outflows. The US objective should be that China adopt macroeconomic and exchange rate policies that would avoid the emergence of a large chronic Chinese global trade surplus position, which would necessarily imply a net reduction of jobs in other countries.

Export Credits

To compete effectively in China with Japanese and European companies, American firms need access to export credits comparable to those offered by their competitors. The Clinton administration in principle has recognized this reality in its proposed National Export Strategy (Trade Promotion Coordinating Committee 1993). That initiative seeks to increase total US exports by almost 50 percent, to reach $1 trillion annually by the year 2000 and to create 6 million new American jobs. But in practice, the initiative falls short in several respects.

First, the proposed funding for the US Eximbank is far too small; indeed, there will be no significant increase at all. The National Export Strategy proposes only a $150 million fund to finance major capital projects abroad. Of this, $50 million will come from the Bank's existing war chest, a special fund used to counter concessional foreign financing. The remaining $100 million is to come from proportional contributions from the export promotion budgets of a number of other US government agencies. Thus the proposal would provide an increase of Eximbank funding of only $100 million, a trivial amount compared with the $12.3 billion in assistance provided to US exporters in fiscal 1992.

The $150 million represents the subsidy component of the fund, which would allow the Bank to make $600 million annually in below-market rate tied-aid credits (General Accounting Office 1993b, 5). These funds are to be used on a worldwide basis. This amount is less than the average annual amount the Japanese Eximbank provided for loans to China alone in 1989–91 (table 3.5b). In addition, the Japanese in their current OECF package are providing an additional $1 billion in aid to China annually. While these funds are nominally untied, as discussed earlier in this chapter, they are used largely to finance the sales of Japanese capital goods to China. The Clinton package does not include any explicit bilateral aid for China comparable to Japan's OECF support.

Second, the program of tied aid credits for major capital projects will not come on stream until the 1995 fiscal year at the earliest.

Finally, the availability of funding for the initiative is uncertain. The proposal does not provide for any increased federal spending but merely calls for a redirection of existing export promotion funds. The redirection to the US Eximbank of existing funds of other agencies, which now go overwhelmingly to support agricultural exports, requires congressional approval. This will be hotly debated.

Export Controls and Sanctions

The most comprehensive study of total US exports foregone on a world-wide basis due to US export disincentives in the mid-1980s produced estimates centering on a range from $21 billion to $27 billion. Export controls for national security accounted for two-thirds to three-quarters of the total. The balance was accounted for by foreign policy sanctions, low levels of official export finance, and regulatory burdens (Richardson 1993, 2–3). Country-by-country estimates of the effect of export disincentives for 1989 placed foregone exports to China at between $5 billion and $10 billion, an amount exceeded only by exports foregone to the Soviet Union. Most of the shortfall in exports to China was in chemicals, industrial machinery, electronic and electrical equipment, transportation equipment, instruments, and related products.

Most interestingly, Richardson estimates that US export shortfalls to China and other countries subject to national security export controls actually rose between 1989 and 1991. This was largely because, compared with other advanced industrial countries, the United States was slow to liberalize or rationalize its export controls. And in the case of China, additional sanctions and controls were imposed after Tiananmen that did not have their full effect until after 1989 (Richardson 1993, 105).

The revision of the Export Administration Act in 1994 offers a unique opportunity to reduce the export disincentives that have been inherent in the system of export controls and sanctions. The Export Administration Act is the single most important law governing US export controls. The 1988 law was to lapse in 1990, but agreement on rewriting the act could not be reached, so it was reauthorized until mid-1994. The act must now be rewritten to reflect the changes in the international security environment since 1988.

The revised act should contain several features. First, the foreign availability principle should be strengthened so that US exporters are not denied foreign sales opportunities when alternative uncontrolled sources of supply are available. At present, licenses can be denied to US exporters for either foreign policy or nonproliferation concerns, even when alternative uncontrolled sources of supply are available. Richardson and others have pointed out that denying export licenses in these cases provides no additional national security and at best is merely an ineffectual symbol of US foreign policy aims. "The United States cannot afford economically costly symbolism, especially when the costs are borne by its most dynamic, technologically competitive sectors" (Richardson 1993, 134–35).

Second, licensing procedures should be streamlined so that license applications are handled more expeditiously. One example demonstrates the cumbersome character of the present system. Beginning as early as 1984, business groups proposed the liberalization of export controls to allow the sale to China of fiber-optic transmission equipment. In particular, AT&T for years has sought unsuccessfully to export high-speed fiber-optic transmission equipment to China and Russia. AT&T estimates that its inability to get an export license has cost the company $100 million annually in lost sales. Finally, in June 1993 it filed a foreign availability petition to demonstrate that the equipment could be supplied by other countries not subject to export controls. But it took six months, until 10 December 1993, for the Department of Commerce to issue a preliminary ruling that the technology the company seeks to export is available from a variety of other uncontrolled sources outside the United States. A final determination was scheduled to be made after allowing 30 days for review of the preliminary decision by the National Security Agency, the Department of Defense, and other intelligence agencies. But the review apparently was not completed as planned since no result had been announced by mid-March 1994.

Third, the new act should require that all export controls, including those designed to limit the spread of weapons of mass destruction, be implemented on a multilateral basis. Although the MTCR, the NSG, and the AG are multilateral organizations, approvals and denials of specific exports are at every nation's discretion (Richardson 1993, 38). Unlike COCOM restrictions on dual-use industrial technology, there appear to be no procedures for implementing the export controls of these other regimes on a multilateral basis.

Two examples demonstrate the increasingly unilateral imposition of controls by the United States under these regimes. First, the proliferation sanctions imposed on China subsequent to the Clinton administration's determination in the fall of 1993 that the Chinese had violated the MTCR were unilateral rather than multilateral. Second, multilateral negotiations among the members of the NSG in 1992 led to a revised list of controlled exports for which validated export licenses are required. Specifically, the NSG agreed to delete equipment, such as steam turbines and generators, from the list. But unlike other members of the NSG, the United States delayed implementation of this multilaterally negotiated reduction in the list of controlled items until March 1994.

The new Export Administration Act should repeal the provision of the National Defense Authorization Act of 1990 that removes discretion and requires that the United States impose sanctions unilaterally in the event of violations of the MTCR. The act also should direct the executive branch of the US government to strengthen the provisions in the MTCR and other multilateral arrangements for controlling nuclear, chemical, and biological items that govern the imposition of multilateral sanctions in the event of violations of these regimes. And finally, it should require that the United States implement on a timely basis changes in the export control lists that are negotiated multilaterally through these control regimes.

The principle of maximum multilateralism dictates that the sanctions the United States imposed on China in 1989 should be lifted at the earliest opportunity. That may require legislative action in some cases. Although many sanctions were first imposed by executive order, for the most part they were formalized by amendments to the Foreign Relations Authorization Act of fiscal 1990–91. Legislative repeal or administrative lifting of these sanctions would allow the resumption of TDA-funded feasibility studies for major infrastructure projects in China and is a prerequisite for the resumption of OPIC programs for US firms making direct investments in China.[13] Less important for US commercial interests, full repeal would also allow the export of both crime control and detection equipment and items on the Munitions Control List. Since other nations either never imposed or have long since dropped limitations on parallel programs and exports, continuation of these controls by the United States simply handicaps US firms that are competing with Japanese and European companies.

Reinstatement of the TDA program in China is also potentially quite important, particularly if the overall funding level for TDA were increased. In the pre-1989 period, this program was one of the most effective in generating US export sales to China.

GATT Participation

The United States should work for China's early entry into the GATT. There is no doubt that the discussions in the working group since 1986, and on a bilateral basis with the United States and other countries over a shorter period, have advanced considerably the reform of China's foreign trade regime. This has clearly been a case where multilateral pressure for reform has been skillfully used by economic reformers within China to advance their own agenda. The danger now is that US leverage for further change in this arena is diminishing. It is time to recognize that the United States has already demanded and received more from China in terms of economic reforms than was demanded of other comparatively developed countries when they entered the GATT.

Since the United States will invoke Article 35 when China enters the GATT, a separate bilateral agreement between the United States and China will be negotiated at the time of entry. The United States should offer to apply the 10-year phaseout of the MFA agreed in the Uruguay Round with respect to China in exchange for the maximum possible tariff concessions and reductions of nontariff barriers by the Chinese.

There is some advantage to China's becoming a participant in the GATT in 1994 so that it may become an original member of the new World Trade Organization (WTO), scheduled to replace the GATT in 1995. Countries that are not already members of the GATT when it expires will have to reapply to participate in the WTO.

Once China is a participant in the GATT, it will be subject to all of the GATT protocols and conventions. And the United States gives up little in terms of subjecting China to future sanctions that are provided for under US trade law. As suggested below, the United States presumably will have to invoke Article 35 so that China will not immediately receive permanent MFN status in the US market. The United States and other

---

13. Reinstatement of OPIC programs in China also requires that agency to make a positive determination on workers' rights in China.

countries will be able to invoke the safeguard clause when China begins to participate in the GATT to counter surges in Chinese exports of specific products. The United States will still, of course, be able to investigate Chinese trade practices under the provisions of Section 301 of the US Trade Act and impose sanctions, if warranted. The US experience in 1991 and 1992 in negotiations with China leading to bilateral agreements on intellectual property protection and market access, discussed in detail in chapter 4, demonstrates that existing US trade legislation provides considerable leverage to US negotiators.[14]

Separation of Human Rights and Other Issues from MFN Status

The United States should provide China permanent MFN status as soon as it is evident that China is in compliance with the protocol governing its participation in the GATT. As already noted in chapter 4, China already is in compliance with the terms of the Jackson-Vanik Amendment to the Trade Act of 1974. This point was acknowledged by the White House when it announced the extension of China's MFN status in the US market for another year beginning in July 1993 (White House press release, 28 May 1993, 1) The flow of Chinese from China to the United States is restricted primarily by US immigration policy, not Chinese emigration policy. On that grounds alone, China should no longer be subject to the annual renewal of its MFN status.

Equally important, reforms of China's domestic economy, discussed in chapter 1, have now proceeded so far that one can at least question whether China falls into the category of a "nonmarket economy" as set forth in the Jackson-Vanik Amendment. As was noted in chapter 1, as of 1993, 95 percent of all retail sales, 90 percent of all sales of agricultural commodities, and even 85 percent of all sales of capital goods in China were at market-determined rather than state-fixed prices. If China no longer falls into the nonmarket economy category, that constitutes yet another reason that MFN should be conferred on a permanent rather than an annual basis.

Because of the legislative history of the Jackson-Vanik Amendment, it is probably not possible to provide China with permanent MFN status

---

14. Critics of the new GATT agreement concluding the Uruguay Round argue that it will undermine the ability of US negotiators to use Section 301 of the US Trade Act of 1974 to ensure foreign market liberalization. USTR disputes this criticism, arguing that it will be able to impose trade sanctions without fear of counterretaliation if countries fail to live up to their obligations. Which perspective is more accurate will probably depend on the details of the enabling legislation that the executive branch must submit to the US Congress.

without congressional action.[15] Thus the United States will invoke Article 35 when China begins to participate in the GATT. However, in return for the final concessions the Chinese offer in the GATT negotiations, the US government should pledge to work both toward the annual renewal of MFN for some interim period and toward the necessary legislative action to repeal the application of the Jackson-Vanik Amendment as it applies to China in order to confer permanent MFN status. The timing and speed of the legislative process should be tied to China's compliance with the terms of the protocol governing its participation in the GATT.

Currency Manipulation Charges

Until there is persuasive evidence that China is undervaluing its currency, thus promoting exports and inhibiting imports, the US Treasury Department should drop its charge that US exports into China are checked by China's manipulation of the exchange rate. Particularly when China is running a global trade deficit, it is hard to sustain an argument that the currency is undervalued. Bilateral negotiations on exchange rate issues might usefully be continued. Treasury might provide valuable advice on China's transition to a currency that would be fully convertible initially on current account and eventually on capital account transactions as well, an announced Chinese objective. But this should be done with the full realization that this likely will lead to a real depreciation of China's currency.

Enhancing the JCCT, JEC, and Other Trade Promotion Activities

The US-China Joint Commission on Commerce and Trade (JCCT) was established in 1983 to ensure high-level attention to bilateral trade and investment issues and to generally promote trade relations between the United States and China. The US secretary of commerce and the Chinese minister of foreign trade and economic relations led the participation of the US and Chinese government delegations, respectively, in the meetings of the JCCT. US participation in what had been the annual meetings of the JCCT was suspended after June 1989. Although Commerce Secretary Barbara Franklin visited China in the waning days of the Bush administration, the JCCT has been moribund. The scheduled April visit of Chinese Trade Minister Wu Yi will provide an opportunity

---

15. Experts consulted on this point had different points of view. Some insisted that the legislative history of the Jackson-Vanik Amendment since it was passed means that legislative action is required. Others insisted that the action technically could be taken by the executive branch.

to revive the JCCT and to begin to develop it into a strong mechanism for anticipating and resolving bilateral trade issues.

The annual meetings of the JCCT should be designed to hasten negotiations on a range of bilateral economic issues. Many of the most contentious issues in these discussions cannot be solved by the working-level staff who have been carrying the negotiating burden. Bringing cabinet-level officials on both sides together on a regular basis could accelerate progress on many issues. The secretary of commerce should also lead major trade and investment delegations to China to advance US commercial interests there.

Similarly, the JEC should become an effective mechanism for dealing with finance, banking, taxation, and other issues. As discussed above, a start has been made by identifying a promising range of issues that will be discussed.

Summary

China poses a unique set of problems, both for the world economy and the United States. Although China is and will remain a low-income developing country, its huge population and its reforming domestic economy make it a much larger participant in world trade and financial markets than any other developing economy. Since political power remains highly centralized under the Chinese Communist Party, it is regarded by many in the West as a historical anomaly in an era when democracy is commonly perceived to be an ascendent international political force. Yet its economy, in certain respects, is already more marketized than some other transforming former socialist states. And the United States confronts a historically unique trade partner—one that has a large and growing bilateral surplus with the United States despite a global trade and current account deficit.

The key recommendation of this study is that international interests are best advanced by facilitating China's further integration into the world economy. This does not mean that China should automatically accede to the GATT or be welcomed as a member of the Organization for Economic Cooperation and Development. The international community must demand appropriate concessions from China, for example, as a condition for its participation in the GATT. Thus, the Chinese must agree to a demanding schedule of reductions of tariffs and quantitative restrictions, such as quotas and other nontariff barriers, and to increase the transparency of its trade system, particularly import decision making. In addition, China will have to accept a safeguard clause in the protocol, allowing existing contracting parties to impose either increased tariffs or quantitative restrictions on Chinese imports in the event that surges in imports cause serious losses for domestic industries. Finally, the protocol will not fully satisfy the Chinese demand that it specifically identify China's participation in the GATT as a resumption. It is much more likely that the final wording will be ambiguous.

China's participation in the OECD and the Group of Seven (G-7) or a successor organization is not yet under active consideration. But Taiwan's campaign to become a member of the OECD may stimulate discussion of China's participation. Since China's trade and capital flows are already approaching the levels of the smaller members, discussion of China's participation in the G-7 eventually may arise as well. Among the most important factors to be considered in both cases should be whether China has complied with the terms of the protocol governing its participation in the GATT. In short, China's participation in these organizations should not be automatic but implicitly conditional upon its ongoing compliance with the norms and expectations of those organizations in which it already participates and the fulfillment of memorandums of understanding and other bilateral agreements that it has signed.

The United States, as the only world economic superpower and China's largest export market, is central to the process of integrating China further into the world economy. US policy toward China, however, appears somewhat ambiguous. On the one hand, the Clinton administration has taken several steps to link the United States more closely to China's rapidly growing economy. On the other hand, the United States is still the only country that does not extend permanent MFN status to China but only extends it on an annual basis, conditional on improvements in human rights conditions. It also is the only country that has imposed sanctions on China for its apparent violations of the MTCR.

The principal recommendations of this study for US policy are to deal with China as a more equal partner and to maximize reliance on multilateral rather than unilateral sanctions where China's behavior falls short of internationally accepted norms. These recommendations are based on several propositions supported by detailed analysis in this study. First, sanctions that impose a higher cost on US exporters than they do on the Chinese government are not viable in the short run and in the long run impose substantial costs in terms of reduced US credibility. The imposition followed by the removal of unilateral US sanctions for asserted Chinese violations of the MTCR is perhaps the best example. The sanctions were imposed in April 1991, removed in March 1992, reimposed in August 1993, and then lifted for a second time in January and March 1994. According to press reports, the actual evidence of Chinese violations of the MTCR was ambiguous. The removal of the sanctions the first time was a response to a Chinese verbal commitment to agree to the provisions of the MTCR. But the partial lifting of sanctions in January and March 1994 appears to have been not in response to any Chinese concessions on proliferation issues, but to have grown out of a concern over potential economic losses that Martin Marietta and

Hughes Aircraft would suffer if sales of communications satellites were lost to other international competitors. The imposition of sanctions, followed by their removal when it appears that US companies are in serious danger of losing substantial sales opportunities, serves no useful purpose and in the long run may corrode the credibility of US participation in the multilateral sanctions regimes recommended in this study.

A close corollary is that Chinese behavior—whether in human rights, nonproliferation, or other areas—that does not meet acceptable international standards is most effectively addressed by multilateral rather than unilateral sanctions. Unilateral sanctions are usually either ineffective or not sustainable. Equally important, repeated US reliance on unilateral sanctions on some issues of importance to the United States makes it more difficult to work cooperatively with the Chinese to solve other bilateral issues.

Third, the United States should work to more systematically integrate China into the world economy. This requires a fundamental change in attitude toward China. Perhaps most important, it requires taking a longer term view than has been the case in the recent past. Already in certain important respects, the Chinese economy is relatively open and integration is well under way. Furthering this process will increase China's stake in the world economy and is likely to increase the likelihood that China will work cooperatively on noneconomic issues as well. Over the longer run, further engagement will accelerate the domestic transformations that are most likely to lead to a more pluralistic political system and ultimately to a more favorable human rights environment as well.

As suggested above, working for China's further integration in the world economy does not mean automatically accommodating all Chinese desires. Rather, it means bargaining hard on the final steps leading to China's participation in the GATT and then providing permanent MFN status if China lives up to the terms of the GATT protocol, as well as the terms of earlier bilateral agreements on market access, intellectual property rights protection, trade in textiles, prison labor exports, and so forth. Such steps are the best way to ensure that China understands that integration implies obligations and responsibilities as well as rights and opportunities.

Appendix

China and the GATT: A Chronology

30 October 1947	The Republic of China signs the Final Act of Geneva that creates the GATT.
21 April 1948	The Republic of China signs the Protocol of Provisional Application for the GATT.
21 May 1948	The Republic of China enters the GATT as a founding member.
6 March 1950	The Republic of China notifies the secretary general of the United Nations of its decision to withdraw from the GATT.
5 May 1950	The withdrawal of the Republic of China takes effect.
16 March 1965	The Republic of China begins to attend GATT meetings as an observer.
19 November 1971	The Republic of China's observer status in GATT meetings is discontinued subsequent to China's admission to the United Nations.
July 1981	China is granted observer status in discussions of the renewal of the Multi-Fiber Arrangement (MFA), a multilateral textile agreement implemented under the auspices of the GATT.

Sources: Cai Wenguo (1992); GATT documents; Jacobson and Oksenberg (1990); Ya Qin (1993).

November 1982	China is granted observer status in the GATT, allowing it to attend the annual meeting of the contracting parties.
November 1983	China again is granted observer status to attend the annual meeting of the contracting parties.
December 1983	China applies to join the MFA.
January 1984	China signs the Arrangement Regarding International Trade in Textiles and is admitted to the MFA.
December 1984	China is granted permanent observer status in the GATT, allowing it to attend meetings of the GATT Council of Representatives.
10 January 1986	The Chinese premier, Zhao Ziyang, in a meeting with Secretary General of the GATT Arthur Dunkel, states China's desire to restore its status in the GATT.
23 April 1986	Hong Kong becomes a contracting party to the GATT under the provisions of Article 26.
11 July 1986	China formally requests resumption of its seat in the GATT.
13 February 1987	China submits a memorandum describing its trade regime, the first step in the process of participating in the GATT.
4 March 1987	The GATT Council decides to appoint a working party on China's status as a contracting party.
June 1987	The GATT appoints the Working Party on China, chaired by Ambassador Pierre-Louis Girard of Switzerland.
February 1988	The first meeting of the Working Party on China takes place.
11–13 July 1989	Scheduled eighth meeting of the Working Party on China is cancelled.
12 December 1989	The eighth meeting of the Working Party on China is held.
1 January 1990	The Republic of China files a formal request to become a participant in the GATT under the provisions of Article 33.
20–21 September 1990	The ninth meeting of the Working Party on China is held.
13–14 February 1991	The tenth meeting of the Working Party on China is held.
29 September 1992	The GATT Council decides to appoint a working party to review the application for membership of Chinese Taipei and restores its observer status in the GATT.

21–23 October 1992	The 11th meeting of the Working Party on China is held.
6 November 1992	The first meeting of the Working Party on the Accession of Chinese Taipei is held.
9–11 December 1992	The 12th meeting of the Working Party on China is held.
15–17 March 1993	The 13th meeting of the Working Party on China is held.
15–16 April 1993	The second meeting of the Working Party on the Accession of Chinese Taipei is held.
24–28 May 1993	The 14th meeting of the Working Party on China is held.
28 June–1 July 1993	The third meeting of the Working Party on the Accession of Chinese Taipei is held.
28–30 September 1993	The 15th meeting of the Working Party on China is held.
12–15 October 1993	The fourth meeting of the Working Party on the Accession of Chinese Taipei is held.
15–18 March 1994	The 16th meeting of the Working Party on China is held.
March 1994	The fifth meeting of the Working Party on the Accession of Chinese Taipei is held.

References

Bergsten, C. Fred, and Marcus Noland. 1993. *Reconcilable Differences? United States–Japan Economic Conflict.* Washington: Institute for International Economics.

Bertsch, Gary K., and Richard T. Cupitt. 1993. "Nonproliferation in the 1990s: Enhancing International Cooperation on Export Controls." *The Washington Quarterly* 16, no. 4 (autumn): 53–70.

Brabant, Jozef M. van. 1991. *The Planned Economies and International Economic Organizations.* Cambridge (UK): Cambridge University Press.

Cai Wenguo. 1992. "China's GATT Membership: Selected Legal and Political Issues." *Journal of World Trade* 26, no. 1 (February): 35–61.

Collins, Susan M., and Dani Rodrik. 1991. *Eastern Europe and the Soviet Union in the World Economy.* Washington: Institute for International Economics.

Department of the Treasury. 1990. *National Treatment Study: Report to the Congress on Foreign Government Treatment of U.S. Commercial Banking and Securities Organizations.* Washington: Department of the Treasury.

Eckstein, Alexander. 1966. *Communist China's Economic Growth and Foreign Trade: Implications for U.S. Policy.* New York: McGraw-Hill.

Encarnation, Dennis J. 1992. *Rivals beyond Trade: America versus Japan in Global Competition.* Ithaca: Cornell University Press.

Ensign, Margee M. 1992. *Doing Good or Doing Well? Japan's Foreign Aid Program.* New York: Columbia University Press.

Harding, Harry. 1992. *A Fragile Relationship: The United States and China since 1972.* Washington: Brookings Institution.

Harrold, Peter. N.d. *China: Enterprise Reform Strategy.* Washington: World Bank. Forthcoming.

Herzstein, Robert E. 1986. "China and the GATT: Legal and Policy Issues Raised by China's Participation in the General Agreement on Tariffs and Trade." *Law and Policy in International Business* 18, no. 2: 371–413.

Igarashi, Masaki. 1989. "Chinese Bonds in the Introduction of Foreign Capital." *JETRO China Newsletter* 82 (September-October): 9–15.

Jacobson, Harold K., and Michel Oksenberg. 1990. *China's Participation in the IMF, the World Bank and GATT: Toward a Global Economic Order*. Ann Arbor: University of Michigan Press.

Kemme, David M. 1991. "Introduction: Technology Controls and Prospects for Change in the 1990s." In D. Kemme, *Technology Markets and Export Controls in the 1990s*. New York: New York University Press.

Khan, Azizur Rahman, Keith Griffin, Carl Riskin, and Zhao Renwei. 1992. "Household Income and Its Distribution in China." *The China Quarterly* 132 (December): 1029–61.

Kravis, Irving B. 1981. "An Approximation of the Relative Real Per Capita GDP of the People's Republic of China." *Journal of Comparative Economics* 5, no. 1 (March): 60–78.

Krause, Lawrence, and Sueo Sekiguchi. 1976. "Japan and the World Economy." In Hugh Patrick and Henry Rosovsky, *Asia's New Giant: How the Japanese Economy Works*. Washington: Brookings Institution.

Lardy, Nicholas R. 1992a. "Chinese Foreign Trade." *The China Quarterly* 131 (September): 691–720.

Lardy, Nicholas R. 1992b. *Foreign Trade and Economic Reform in China, 1978–1990*. Cambridge (UK): Cambridge University Press.

Lardy, Nicholas R. 1993. "China as a NIC." *International Economic Insights* 4, no. 3 (May/June): 5–7.

Ma Guonan and Ross Garnaut. 1992. *How Rich Is China: Evidence from the Food Economy*. Working Papers in Trade and Development No. 92/4. Canberra: The Australian National University, Research School of Pacific Studies.

Niu Genying. 1994. "China's Economic Reform in 1994." *Beijing Review* 37, no. 2 (10–16 January): 10–12.

Palmeter, N. David. 1989. "The Impact of the U.S. Antidumping Law on China-U.S. Trade." *Journal of World Trade* 23, no. 4 (August): 1–14.

Patrick, Hugh, and Henry Rosovsky. 1976. "Japan's Economic Performance: An Overview." In Hugh Patrick and Henry Rosovsky, *Asia's New Giant: How the Japanese Economy Works*. Washington: Brookings Institution.

Pearson, Margaret M. 1991. *Joint Ventures in the People's Republic of China: The Control of Foreign Direct Investment under Socialism*. Princeton: Princeton University Press.

Perkins, Dwight H. 1992. "China's Economic Boom and the Integration of the Economies of East Asia." Unpublished manuscript (October).

Preeg, Ernest H. 1993. "The Aid for Trade Debate." *The Washington Quarterly* 16, no.1 (winter): 99–114.

Qian Yingyi. 1993. "Lessons and Relevance of the Japanese Main Bank System for Financial System Reform in China." Unpublished manuscript (May).

Richardson, J. David. 1993. *Sizing Up U.S. Export Disincentives*. Washington: Institute for International Economics.

SaKong, Il. 1993. *Korea in the World Economy*. Washington: Institute for International Economics.

Segal, Gerald. 1993. "The Coming Confrontation between China and Japan?" *World Policy Journal* 10, no. 2 (summer): 27–32.

Summers, Robert, and Alan Heston. 1988. "A New Set of International Comparisons of Real Product and Prices Levels: Estimates for 130 Countries, 1950–1985." *Review of Income and Wealth* 34, no. 1 (March): 1–25.

Summers, Robert, and Alan Heston. 1991. "An Expanded Set of International Comparisons, 1950–1988." *Quarterly Journal of Economics* 106, no. 2 (May): 327–68.

Sung Yun-wing. 1991a. "Foreign Trade and Investment." In *China Review 1990*. Hong Kong: The Chinese University Press.

Sung Yun-wing. 1991b. *The China–Hong Kong Connection: The Key to China's Open-Door Policy*. Cambridge (UK): Cambridge University Press.

Taylor, Jeffrey. 1991. *Dollar GNP Estimates for China*. Center for International Research Staff Paper No. 59. Washington: United States Bureau of the Census (March).

Trade Promotion Coordinating Committee. 1993. *Toward a National Export Strategy.* Washington (30 September).

Tsao, James T. H. 1987. *China's Development Strategies and Foreign Trade.* Lexington, MA: Lexington Books.

US General Accounting Office. 1990. *Export Controls: Advising U.S. Business of Policy Changes.* Washington: GAO.

US General Accounting Office. 1993a. *Export Controls: Issues in Removing Militarily Sensitive Items from the Munitions List.* Washington: GAO.

US General Accounting Office. 1993b. *Export Finance: Challenges Facing the U.S. Export-Import Bank.* Washington: GAO.

Vogel, Ezra. 1989. *One Step Ahead in China: Guangdong Under Reform.* Cambridge, MA: Harvard University Press.

World Bank. 1992a. *China: Strategies for Reducing Poverty in the 1990s.* Washington: World Bank.

World Bank. 1992b. *China: Reform and the Role of the Plan in the 1990s.* Washington: World Bank.

World Bank. 1993a. *China Foreign Trade Reform: Meeting the Challenge of the 1990s.* Washington: World Bank.

World Bank. 1993b. *China Updating Economic Memorandum: Managing Rapid Growth and Transition.* Washington: World Bank.

World Bank. 1993c. *The East Asian Miracle: Economic Growth and Public Policy.* New York: Oxford University Press.

World Bank. 1993d. *Economic Trends in Developing Countries.* Washington: World Bank.

World Bank. 1993e. *World Debt Tables: External Finance for Developing Countries.* Washington: World Bank.

World Bank. 1993f. *China: Urban Land Management in an Emerging Market Economy.* Washington: World Bank.

Ya Qin. 1993. "China and GATT: Accession Instead of Resumption." *Journal of World Trade* 27, no. 2 (April): 77–98.

Yang Deming. 1992. "A Study of China's Foreign Economic Development Strategy." *Guoji maoyi* (International Trade) no. 11 (November): 7–13.

Yukawa Kazuo. 1992. "Economic Cooperation between Guangdong and Inland Areas." *JETRO China Newsletter* 100 (September-October): 9–16.

Zhao Cao. 1993. "Foreign Funded Enterprises Have Become a Fresh Force in Exports." *Guoji shangbao* (International Business) 8 July, p. 1.

Index

Hong Kong participation, 47, 77n
requirements for membership, 44
Soviet participation, 6
Working Party on China, 106
General Electric Company, 98
Generalized System of Preferences (GSP), 44
Geneva Phonograms Convention, 80
Giordano, 66
GNP. *See* Gross national product (GNP)
Golden Venture, 100
Grant funds, 58
Greater China, US trade deficit with, 78, 79t
Gross domestic product (GDP), estimates of, 14–18, 15t
Gross national product (GNP)
estimates of, 18
growth in, 3
ratio of exports to, 39
GSP. *See* Generalized System of Preferences
Guangdong International Trust and Investment Corporation, 60
Guangdong Investment Limited, 61
Guangdong Province, economy of, 26–27
Guangdong provincial government, investments, 27
Guangzhou Iron and Steel Co. Ltd., 65t
Guangzhou Peugeot Automobile, 65t

Hard currency exports, 5n
Hong Kong
accession to GATT, 47, 77n
Chinese investment in, 114
Chinese reexports to US through, 75–77, 76t
customs, 77n
effects of discontinuing China's MFN status on, 101–102
imports from US, 117, 118t
investment in China, 71
participation in GATT, 77n
role in US-China trade, 75
trade deficit with US, 78, 79t
trade with China, 34
Hong Kong Aircraft Engineering Company (HAECO), 68
Hong Kong International Terminals, 69
Hong Kong Stock Exchange, Chinese companies listing on, 62–63
Hopewell Holdings, 67–68
Huaqiang Sanyo Electronics Co., Ltd., 65t
Hughes Aircraft Company, 97, 125
Human rights, 126, 136–137
Hunan Province, economy of, 26
Hutchison Whampoa, 69
Hydropower development, 27, 67–68

IBRD. *See* International Bank for Reconstruction and Development
ICP. *See* International Comparison Project
IDA. *See* International Development Association

IFC. *See* International Finance Corporation
IIL. *See* International Industrial List
IMF. *See* International Monetary Fund
Import quotas, 42–43
Imports
commodity composition of, 32–33
by foreign-invested firms, 116n
from Japan, 122–123
restrictions, 81–83, 92–97
subsidized, 10
from US, 75, 76t, 92–97, 117, 118t
India
loans to, 52–53
role in world economy, 27–8
Insurance
joint ventures, 70
US firms in China, 91
Intellectual property rights protection, 79–81
International Bank for Reconstruction and Development (IBRD), loans to China, 50, 51t, 52
International capital markets, Chinese participation in, 49–79, 105
International Comparison Project (ICP), 16
International Development and Finance Act of 1989, 122
International Development Association (IDA), 50, 51t, 52, 105
International Finance Corporation (IFC), 52
International Industrial List (IIL), 93–94
International Intellectual Property Alliance, 80
International Monetary Fund (IMF), 4, 6
estimates of China's GDP, 14–17, 15t
International organizations, loans to China, 50–54
International trade, Eastern European participation in, 5–7
International Trade Commission. *See* United States International Trade Commission
Investment. *See* Foreign direct investment
ITC. *See* United States International Trade Commission

Jackson-Vanik amendment. *See* Trade Act of 1974
Japan, 119–124
assistance to China, 54–58, 57t, 120, 122–123
economic growth, 4
equity markets, 115
export credits, 58, 122
exports to China, 122–123
foreign-invested firms in, 112
foreign investment in, 111
imports from China, 123
investment in China, 124, 125t
nontariff barriers, 42, 43t
official development assistance to China, 56–58, 57t
official export credits to China, 58

People's Insurance Company of China (PICC), 70, 91
Per capita income, 4
  estimates, 15*t*, 17–18
Per capita output, 107
  estimates, 24–25
PICC. *See* People's Insurance Company of China
PlanEcon, 5*n*
Poland
  exports, 5, 28, 28*n*
  participation in international trade, 5–7
Port development, foreign investment in, 69
Power generation, foreign investment in, 67–68
Price controls, 8–11, 11*t*
  currency, 87
Prices, effects of discontinuing China's MFN status on, 102
Prison labor exports, 98–99
Processed exports, 112–114, 113*t*
Proliferation sanctions, 96–97, 134–135

Railroads, 68–69
Reexports, to US, 75–77, 76*t*
Renminbi, 1*n*
  convertibility of, 3, 106
  devaluation of, 37, 90
  price controls, 87
  purchasing power of, 3, 16
    estimates of China's GDP based on, 14–17, 15*t*
Retail commodities, price controls, 10, 11*t*
Retailing, foreign investment in, 66–67
Rockwell International, 97
Royal Dutch Shell, 70

Salomon Brothers, 62
Sanctions, 54, 55*t*, 81, 119, 132–135, 140
  proliferation, 96–98, 125–126, 134–135
Sanwa, 61
Sealand, 91–92
Securities sales, 58–63
Services, 70–71, 90–92
Shajiao B power plant, 67
Shajiao C power plant, 67
Shangdong Provincial Electric Power Bureau, 68
Shanghai Bell Telephone Equipment Co., Ltd., 65*t*
Shanghai Container Terminals, 69
Shanghai International Trust and Investment Corporation, 60
Shanghai Petrochemical Co. Ltd., 62
Shanghai securities market, 115
Shanghai stock exchange, 62
Shanghai Volkswagen AG, 65*t*
Shattuck, John, 126
Shenyang Jinbei Bus Manufacturing Co. Ltd., 65*t*

Shenzhen Konka Electronics (Group) Co. Ltd., 65*t*
Shenzhen securities market, 115
Shenzhen stock exchange, 62
Shenzhen Zhonghua Bicycles (Group) Co. Ltd., 65*t*
Shipping, US-China agreement, 91–92
Siemens, 69
Singapore, US exports to, 117, 118*t*
Singapore Airline Engineering Co. Ltd., 68
Sino-Japanese Friendship Hospital, 58
Sinotrans, 92
Smoot-Hawley tariffs, 98
SOEs. *See* State-owned enterprises
South China Joint Hydropower Company, 27
South Korea
  foreign-invested firms in, 112
  foreign investment in, 111
  investment in China, 71
  trade deficit with US, 129
  US exports to, 117, 118*t*
Soviet Union
  exports to market economies, 4, 5*n*
  foreign investment in, 5
  participation in GATT, 6
  participation in international trade, 6
  trade with China, 33
State-owned enterprises (SOEs), productivity growth, 22
Summers, Lawrence, 86
Sun Hung Kai Property, 67
Swap market rates, 86
Swire Pacific Ltd., 68

Taiwan
  equity markets, 115
  foreign-invested firms in, 112
  foreign investment in, 111
  investment in China, 71
  participation in GATT, 44, 46–47
  trade deficit with US, 78, 79*t*, 129
  US exports to, 117, 118*t*
Takeshita, Noboru, 56
Tariff Act of 1930, 98
Tariffs, 42.
  effects of discontinuing China's MFN status on, 102
  reduction benefits to China, 43–44
  Smoot-Hawley, 98
TDA. *See* Trade and Development Agency
TDP. *See* Trade and Development Program
Technology exports, controls and sanctions on, 92–97, 125–126
Teikoku Oil Co. Ltd., 70
Texaco, 70
Textile trade, 83–86
  country-of-origin rules, 84
  Operation Q-Tip, 84
  US-China agreements, 83–85
Thermal power development, 67–68

Tiananmen massacre, 50–54, 55t, 60, 119
Tianjin International Trust and Investment
 Corporation, 60
Tianshengqiao Hydropower Plant, 27
Trade
 based on comparative advantage, 108
 foreign, 29–47, 30t
 future expansion, 37–44
 goods pricing, 10–11
 implications of investment for, 71
 international, 5–7
 merchandise, 1–3, 2t
 patterns, 33–35, 108
 terms of, 41, 41t
 in textiles, 83–86
 world, 1–4, 2t, 7, 27–47
Trade Act of 1974
 Jackson-Vanik amendment, 44, 99–100, 137n,
  136–137, 477
 Section 301, 80–81
 Section 406, 83–86
Trade Act of 1988, 86
Trade and Development Agency (TDA), 120n,
 121
Trade and Development Program (TDP),
 120–122
Trade credits, 59, 59t. See also Export credits
 short-term, 1
Trademark Law, 80–81
Trade ratio, estimates of, 18
Trade secrets, protection for, 81
Transportation
 civil air, 92
 foreign investment in, 68–69
 prices, 9–10

Unfair competition law, 81
UNICEF, 54
United Nations, 54
United Nations Development Programme
 (UNDP), 54
United States. See also specific administration,
 president
 assistance to China, 50–52, 120–122
 country-of-origin rules, 84
 export controls, 92–97, 132–135
 export growth, 117, 118t
 exports to China, 75, 76t, 92–97, 117, 118t
  reexports through Hong Kong, 75–77, 76t
 immigration to, 100–101
 implications of Chinese openness for,
  117–119
 imports from China, 102
 investment in China, 118–119, 119t, 124,
  124n
 nontariff barriers, 42–43, 43t
 Operation Q-Tip, 84
 policy toward China, 7–8
  objectives of, 90–91
  recommendations, 124–140

strategy of enlargement, 7–8
sanctions against China, 96–97, 132–135
trade balance with China, 34, 73–79, 74t, 76t,
 108–109, 129–131
commodity composition of, 75
effects of discontinuing China's MFN status
 on, 101–103
textile, 81–83
trade deficit with Greater China, 78, 79t
trade deficit with Japan, 109
trade deficit with South Korea, 129
trade deficit with Taiwan, 129
United States Agency for International
 Development, assistance to China, 120
United States banks, in China, 91
United States—China Bilateral Trade
 Agreement, 79
United States—China relations
 aviation agreement, 92
 economic issues, 73–103
 intellectual property rights agreement, 79–81
 Joint Commission on Commerce and Trade,
  80, 137–138
 Joint Economic Commission, 126, 138
 legacy of sanctions, 97–98
 maritime agreement, 91–92
 market access agreement, 81–83
 prison labor agreement, 98–99
 textile agreement, 83–85
United States Export-Import Bank. See Export-
 Import Bank of the United States
United States Immigration Act of 1990, 100
United States Munitions List (USML), 92–93
United States International Trade Commission
 (ITC), 83
United States Trade and Development
 Program, 97
United States Trade Representative (USTR),
 81
Universal Copyright Convention, 80
Universal Declaration of Human Rights, 126
Uruguay Round, 43–44
USML. See United States Munitions List
USTR. See United States Trade Representative

Vietnam Airlines, 95

Westinghouse, 98
Working Party for China, 44
World Bank
 estimates of China's GDP, 14–15, 15t
 loans to China, 1, 3, 49–52, 105
 loans to Eastern European countries, 6
World exports
 China's share, 2
 growth of, 37, 38f
World Food Program, 53
World Health Organization, 53
World trade, China's share, 1–4, 2t, 7, 27–47

Other Publications from the
Institute for International Economics

POLICY ANALYSES IN INTERNATIONAL ECONOMICS Series

1 **The Lending Policies of the International Monetary Fund**
John Williamson/*August 1982*
ISBN paper 0-88132-000-5   72 pp.

2 **"Reciprocity": A New Approach to World Trade Policy?**
William R. Cline/*September 1982*
ISBN paper 0-88132-001-3   41 pp.

3 **Trade Policy in the 1980s**
C. Fred Bergsten and William R. Cline/*November 1982*
(out of print)   ISBN paper 0-88132-002-1   84 pp.
Partially reproduced in the book *Trade Policy in the 1980s.*

4 **International Debt and the Stability of the World Economy**
William R. Cline/*September 1983*
ISBN paper 0-88132-010-2   134 pp.

5 **The Exchange Rate System, Second Edition**
John Williamson/*September 1983, rev. June 1985*
(out of print)   ISBN paper 0-88132-034-X   61 pp.

6 **Economic Sanctions in Support of Foreign Policy Goals**
Gary Clyde Hufbauer and Jeffrey J. Schott/*October 1983*
ISBN paper 0-88132-014-5   109 pp.

7 **A New SDR Allocation?**
John Williamson/*March 1984*
ISBN paper 0-88132-028-5   61 pp.

8 **An International Standard for Monetary Stabilization**
Ronald I. McKinnon/*March 1984*
ISBN paper 0-88132-018-8   108 pp.

9 **The Yen/Dollar Agreement: Liberalizing Japanese Capital Markets**
Jeffrey A. Frankel/*December 1984*
ISBN paper 0-88132-035-8   86 pp.

10 **Bank Lending to Developing Countries: The Policy Alternatives**
C. Fred Bergsten, William R. Cline, and John Williamson/*April 1985*
ISBN paper 0-88132-032-3   221 pp.

11 **Trading for Growth: The Next Round of Trade Negotiations**
Gary Clyde Hufbauer and Jeffrey J. Schott/*September 1985*
ISBN paper 0-88132-033-1   109 pp.

12 **Financial Intermediation Beyond the Debt Crisis**
Donald R. Lessard and John Williamson/*September 1985*
ISBN paper 0-88132-021-8   130 pp.

13 **The United States-Japan Economic Problem**
C. Fred Bergsten and William R. Cline/*October 1985, 2d ed. January 1987*
(out of print)   ISBN paper 0-88132-060-9   180 pp.

BOOKS

Economic Sanctions Reconsidered (in two volumes)
Economic Sanctions Reconsidered: Supplemental Case Histories
Gary Clyde Hufbauer, Jeffrey J. Schott, and Kimberly Ann Elliott/*1985, 2d ed.*
December 1990

ISBN cloth 0-88132-115-X	928 pp.
ISBN paper 0-88132-105-2	928 pp.

Economic Sanctions Reconsidered: History and Current Policy
Gary Clyde Hufbauer, Jeffrey J. Schott, and Kimberly Ann Elliott/*December 1990*

ISBN cloth 0-88132-136-2	288 pp.
ISBN paper 0-88132-140-0	288 pp.

Pacific Basin Developing Countries: Prospects for the Future
Marcus Noland/*January 1991*

ISBN cloth 0-88132-141-9	250 pp.
ISBN paper 0-88132-081-1	250 pp.

Currency Convertibility in Eastern Europe
John Williamson, editor/*October 1991*

ISBN cloth 0-88132-144-3	396 pp.
ISBN paper 0-88132-128-1	396 pp.

Foreign Direct Investment in the United States
Edward M. Graham and Paul R. Krugman/*1989, 2d ed. October 1991*

ISBN paper 0-88132-139-7	200 pp.

International Adjustment and Financing: The Lessons of 1985-1991
C. Fred Bergsten, editor/*January 1992*

ISBN paper 0-88132-112-5	336 pp.

North American Free Trade: Issues and Recommendations
Gary Clyde Hufbauer and Jeffrey J. Schott/*April 1992*

ISBN cloth 0-88132-145-1	392 pp.
ISBN paper 0-88132-120-6	392 pp.

American Trade Politics
I. M. Destler/*1986, 2d ed. June 1992*

ISBN cloth 0-88132-164-8	400 pp.
ISBN paper 0-88132-188-5	400 pp.

Narrowing the U.S. Current Account Deficit
Allen J. Lenz/*June 1992*

ISBN cloth 0-88132-148-6	640 pp.
ISBN paper 0-88132-103-6	640 pp.

The Economics of Global Warming
William R. Cline/*June 1992*

ISBN cloth 0-88132-150-8	416 pp.
ISBN paper 0-88132-132-X	416 pp.

U.S. Taxation of International Income: Blueprint for Reform
Gary Clyde Hufbauer, assisted by Joanna M. van Rooij/*October 1992*

ISBN cloth 0-88132-178-8	304 pp.
ISBN paper 0-88132-134-6	304 pp.

Who's Bashing Whom? Trade Conflict in High-Technology Industries
Laura D'Andrea Tyson/*November 1992*

ISBN cloth 0-88132-151-6	352 pp.
ISBN paper 0-88132-106-0	352 pp.

Korea in the World Economy
Il SaKong/*January 1993*
ISBN cloth 0-88132-184-2   328 pp.
ISBN paper 0-88132-106-0   328 pp.

Pacific Dynamism and the International Economic System
C. Fred Bergsten and Marcus Noland, editors/*May 1993*
ISBN paper 0-88132-196-6   424 pp.

Economic Consequences of Soviet Disintegration
John Williamson, editor/*May 1993*
ISBN paper 0-88132-190-7   664 pp.

Reconcilable Differences? United States-Japan Economic Conflict
C. Fred Bergsten and Marcus Noland/*June 1993*
ISBN paper 0-88132-129-X   296 pp.

Does Foreign Exchange Intervention Work?
Kathryn M. Dominguez and Jeffrey A. Frankel/*September 1993*
ISBN paper 0-88132-104-4   192 pp.

Sizing Up U.S. Export Disincentives
J. David Richardson/*September 1993*
ISBN paper 0-88132-107-9   192 pp.

NAFTA: An Assessment
Gary Clyde Hufbauer and Jeffrey J. Schott/*rev. ed. October 1993*
ISBN paper 0-88132-199-0   216 pp.

Adjusting to Volatile Energy Prices
Philip K. Verleger, Jr./*November 1993*
ISBN paper 0-88132-069-2   288 pp.

The Political Economy of Policy Reform
John Williamson, editor/*January 1994*
ISBN paper 0-88132-195-8   624 pp.

Measuring the Costs of Protection in the United States
Gary Clyde Hufbauer and Kimberly Ann Elliott/*January 1994*
ISBN paper 0-88132-108-7   144 pp.

The Dynamics of Korean Economic Development
Cho Soon/*March 1994*
ISBN paper 0-88132-162-1   272 pp.

Reviving the European Union
C. Randall Henning, Eduard Hochreiter and Gary Clyde Hufbauer/*April 1994*
ISBN paper 0-88132-208-3   192 pp.

China in the World Economy
Nicholas R. Lardy/*April 1994*
ISBN paper 0-88132-200-8   192 pp.

SPECIAL REPORTS

1   **Promoting World Recovery: A Statement on Global Economic Strategy by Twenty-six Economists from Fourteen Countries**/*December 1982*
(out of print)   ISBN paper 0-88132-013-7   45 pp.

FORTHCOMING

For orders outside the US and Canada please contact:

Longman Group UK Ltd.
PO Box 88
Harlow, Essex CM 19 5SR
UK

Telephone Orders: 0279 623925
Fax: 0279 453450
Telex: 817484